The Liverpool Docklands: Life and Work in Athol Street

by

Pat Ayers

First published by Docklands History Project 1987. Reprinted 1988 and 1989.
This edition published 1999 by Liver Press, 14 Appin Road, Birkenhead, Wirral, Merseyside CH41 9HH.

British Library Cataloguing in Publication Data.
A catalogue record for this book is available from the British Library.

ISBN 1 871201 07 1

To
Marie Owens (born Holden)
who so valued other people's memories and
left us the sweetest ones of herself

and

Tony Lee
A warm and truly gentle man
whose early death has been such a great loss
to the community he grew up in

Contents

Illustrations

Illustrations are by courtesy of the following: Frank and Joan Boyce (Photos 23, 24), J. Cusack (Photos 1, 2), Mrs. Dillon (Photos 32,33), Alice Gillon (Photos 9, 29), Mrs. K. Harkins (Photos cover, 6, 15, 17, 18, 19, 26, 27), Liverpool City Engineers Department (Photos 4, 14, 21, back cover), Liverpool Record Office (Photo 5), Liverpool Water Sports Centre (Photo 7), Merseyside Police (Photo 28), the 40th Jewel, compiled by Mr. H. C. Beasley, published by Fr. D., J. Kelly, 1949, (Photos 25, 31, 34), Mrs. M. Walsh (Photos 3, 8, 12, 20, 35). Warmest thanks to you all. Particular thanks to Mr. Ian Green of Liverpool City Engineers Department for unfailing courtesy and prompt response to all my enquiries. Also to Phil Saunders for cover design.

Preface

The Docklands History Project was based in the Departments of Economic and Social History and Sociology at the University of Liverpool from 1986 until the end of its funding in 1990. The Project emerged out of a recognition that the history of Merseyside is inseparable from the history of the people who lived and worked in the dockland areas. During its life, the Project workers - Pat Ayers, Gail Cameron, Alan Johnson and Kevin Moore - collected and preserved photographs and memories of dockland communities. They produced exhibitions, held reunions and worked hard to involve the people they worked with in the recovery and presentation of their own history. The collection put together is now held by National Museums and Galleries on Merseyside and will provide a resource for generations to come.

The Liverpool Docklands: Life and Work in Athol Street, was the first of four booklets published by Docklands History Project. The response to it was overwhelming and it was twice reprinted. Copies were sent to exiles in Africa, Canada, Australia and America and, nearer home, to Ireland and addresses throughout Britain. Families who originated in the area welcomed it into their homes but the book also struck a chord with people who had no connection with Athol Street. It became clear from the reaction to it, that the book reflected experiences which were common also to other dockland communities and to areas throughout the city. In the time since, requests for the book have continued. In response, Liver Press have agreed to make it once again available as part of their History and Society of Merseyside Series.

Liver Press is a joint venture between the Faculty of Social and Environmental Studies at the University of Liverpool, the School of Humanities and Social Science at John Moores University and Countyvise Ltd., publishers of studies in local history. Liver Press was created to publish research material generated within the two universities but of interest to a readership throughout Merseyside and beyond. It has been successful in this and in strengthening links between the two institutions and the local community. In acknowledging the help and support of those without whom this book would never originally, have been written, initial thanks have to go to the Leverhulme Trust for the funding which made the study possible. In addition, I am grateful to National Museums and Galleries on Merseyside and to the University of Liverpool for material support. It is impossible for me to mention individually all those who gave me help during the research for this book but to you all, many thanks. In particular, I am grateful to my co-workers, Gail Cameron and Kevin Moore for their support and encouragement. Also to Alan Johnson whose strength, intellect and sheer presence underpinned the whole Docklands History Project and whose generosity of spirit towards me never failed, even when pushed to the limits of his patience. I remain thankful for the supportive love, friendship and academic stringency of Val Burton and Marij van Helmund. I am grateful to Susan Yee and Ian Qualtrough of the Photographic Unit at the University of Liverpool for all their excellent work. Thanks also to Joseph Cusack for his interest and prompt response to requests for help and to Fr. Byrne, late of St. Alban's church, for his invaluable support and the occasional use of his sitting-room. More immediately, I am grateful to the committee of Liver Press for making the book available again and in particular to John Emmerson of Countyvise Ltd. and to my dear friend, the long-suffering Eric Taplin, whose persistence eventually pushed me into getting the package ready for printing. Thank you also to Helen Threllfall of the Record Centre at the Maritime Museum for her courtesy, efficiency and help in relocating the photographs reproduced here and to Kate Lyons for lending again those taken by her great grandfather. In addition, I owe warmest thanks to all of you who have continued to badger various members of staff at the Department of Economic and Social History at the University of Liverpool, for copies of 'the Athol Street book'. It is your continued interest over the last six years, which convinced people that re-publication would be worthwhile.

Most especially, I owe a great debt to the many men and women who have shared their very precious memories with me and who have loaned photographs. Although I cannot name you all, the following people were particularly giving of their time and interest: Mr. T. Bunner of Bunner Galvanising Services, Mary Dillon, Ivy Griffin, Hughie and Peggy Holden, Jimmy McCarty, Frank and Joan Boyce, Danny and Alice Gillon, Mrs. K. Harkins, Joe Kinsella, Pat McGivern.

1 Grass Between the Cobblestones

> "I came over the bridge and...oh my God, it was like a desert - there's grass, a foot high, growing up between the cobbles, grass! Nothing passes over it now - the street - so grass can grow. No people about, no children playing, just silent like a desert . . . and grass between the cobbles."

Bewilderment, disbelief and a great sense of sadness pervade an elderly man's description of his return to the dockland area where he grew up, after an absence of almost fifty years. The boarded up windows of the tower block, the empty, vandalised and grafitti covered houses and shops of the hopeful 1960s and the abandoned expanse of the gas work's site, seem to offer no sense of the world that was Over the Bridge in the years before the Second World War. Nevertheless, in the early part of 1987, when the news broke that the City Council was to demolish the whole area and relocate the people elsewhere, an action committee was quickly formed to represent the interests of those who wanted to stay.

Many of the families who lived there then had been there for several generations. The post-war slum clearance strategy for Over the Bridge was carried out in such a way that most of the families still living there at that time were rehoused very close to their original homes. In the time between 'strangers' have moved in and the area has become increasingly run down. However, despite the apparent desolation of the surroundings people have invested money, time and energy in creating comfortable homes. More importantly, a deeply-rooted sense of belonging and the security of 'being known' offered its own safety net born of generations of mutual support and give and take.

Looking down from Athol Street bridge.

Much has been written about the past prosperity of the port of Liverpool, of docks filled with ships, streets teeming with traffic, and port-related industries which generated economic success and employment. We still know relatively little, however, about the mass of the population of Liverpool upon whom that prosperity was built. Whether in fictional accounts or in history books, dockland areas have tended to be portrayed in two ways; as warm, close knit, crime free 'poor but happy' districts or as slumland centres of material and cultural deprivation. At best this sort of portrayal offers an idealised vision of a past golden age which might be quite different from reality. At worst, it disguises a huge diversity of experience across time and according to age, status, class, religion, race and gender. By using the memories and voices of the people themselves this study aims to redress the balance enabling us to glimpse the reality of life and work in a dockland community and how this changed over time.

Essentially, the area concerned comprises the streets and courts located in and around Athol Street. Athol Street is situated in the north end of Liverpool and runs down between Scotland Road and Great Howard Street. Although intersected by Vauxhall Road and the viaduct which carries the Liverpool to Southport railway line, it is the Leeds/Liverpool canal which provides the main divide and sets apart the area over the bridge from the top end - a division which endures both for those who still live there and in the memories of those who have left : "If they said, 'Where do you live?' you said, 'Over the Bridge'."

Over the Bridge is the main focus of this work but it can't be seen in isolation from the Top End nor from the adjoining parishes of St. Gerard Majella and St. Augustine's. In many ways, of course, Over the Bridge is very like other dockland areas. People generally saw themselves as part of a particular locality often identifying this around parish, school or industry. All the basic needs of family, work, education, shopping, leisure and health care, were provided in the immediate area so there was little need for people to travel outside the security of familiar neighbourhoods. On top of this there was an expectation that children born and reared Over the Bridge would stay there after they left school, went to work and married: "You stayed in your own community . . . it was a sacrilege to marry out of Over the Bridge." Local people still speak in awe of a couple who married before the War and moved away:

> "I never could understand it, why they did that. He'd been abroad and all that but they belonged down here I mean they'd not, especially her, known different. I still think they took a chance. "

The couple themselves didn't find it easy once they'd made the move

> "We were isolated then, nobody spoke to us, we were like interlopers. Everybody came out in the morning, did their steps, they had these little dust caps on . . . and [did] the brass knockers and knobs, that was it - they shut their doors. We were used to everybody talking, the people out sitting on the steps .

Another couple moved away when first married up to the south end of the city near friends of the woman's but soon returned. The husband recalls:

> "Oh yes, I didn't like it . . . We stuck it a few months and then I said 'Now, I'd rather go back down Over the Bridge.' So I coaxed her to move in with my Dad."

If people weren't expected to move away, neither were newcomers expected to move in. 'Outsiders' remained outsiders in collective memories even twenty or thirty years after they had come to live in the area:

> "Over the Bridge my mother was never accepted . . . I remember just before we left in about 1965, she had a big row with . . . in the street and she said, 'Eh well, you were never welcome here anyway, you up-the-road tart.' "

Even within somewhere as identifiable as Over the Bridge, though, there were other territorial divisions: "If you came from the other side of the [railway] arches, you weren't in the same league as us." Despite children attending school together, when home they tended to play with children from their own and immediately surrounding streets:

> "We always stayed in our own vicinity, like, Barmouth Street, Menai Street, Idris Street, Snowdon Street, we all mixed more or less together. Never went down to [the other side of the arches]. We went to school with them all but we never mixed with them out."

Rivalries between streets or groups of streets were common, finding expression in the relative and much disputed quality of the street decorations at festival times and in the street football teams which became a marked feature of local life. For children, street loyalties might well take on a more physical aspect:

> "Streets were self-contained. We used to have fights with children from Vescock Street and they used to come and raid us, but you'd never get to know them very well."

The Second World War brought sudden and radical change to the north end, but change was clearly inevitable even before 1939. Concern about the very poor quality of housing in the Athol Street area had led to the

New housing at the top end.

development of a number of slum clearance schemes. Plans were dramatically interrupted by the outbreak of War and the destruction begun by German bombing was completed by the City Council in the post-war redevelopment programmes.

The 'new' housing of the 1960s has lasted only the space of one generation. At the top end of Athol Street, well designed, attractive houses are replacing run-down flats and maisonettes. But still, some of the older residents of Over the Bridge were not convinced that they would be gaining more than they were losing if the area was demolished and they were rehoused:

> "If they knock all this down it'll be like when they flooded all those ancient monuments in Egypt to build that dam. Everything'll be swept away, not just the buildings, everything that goes with it . . . and you can't help but ask yourself what it was all about?"

Looking down from the bridge today there doesn't seem to be any easy answer to that question. The lives of the men and women of the dockland communities have always been inextricably tied up with political and economic factors beyond their control. Their share of the port's past prosperity was negligible but many feel that the port's decline has taken away their future. Their memories stand as a tangible tribute to the contribution they made generation after generation, and can help us to rebuild, in words and photographs, the community that was - in the time before grass grew up between the cobblestones.

2 The Growth of the North End Docklands

By 1900, the north end of Liverpool was one of the most important districts in the country. Numerous industries associated with shipping and the processing of imported raw materials were located there. These included ship repair, animal feedstuffs, sugar refining, tobacco, timber, molasses, flourmills, margarine manufacture and a whole host of others. The area was also one of the poorest, most squalid and disease ridden places in Britain.

In response to a rapidly expanding population's demand for gas, Athol Street Gas Works opened in 1834. It was ideally located on the banks of the Leeds-Liverpool canal which provided a direct link with the Wigan coalfield. By 1881, the area had largely taken on the shape it was to retain until the Second World War. The Welsh builders who erected the houses between 1830 and 1870, left evidence of their identity in the street names which survived them, Menai, Snowdon, Cemeas . . . Usually, these houses remained in Welsh hands; local people recall inter-war landlords as being of Welsh extraction. Houses were mainly two and three bedroomed terraces with cellars, small back yards and outside taps and toilets. When newly built each provided adequate accommodation for a single family. Soon though, population increase accompanied by a desperate demand for housing brought a rapid deterioration of conditions.

Since the beginnings of her growth, Liverpool had attracted immigrants in search of work or increasingly, passing through on their way to new areas of settlement abroad. Census returns for the nineteenth century show the population of Athol Street had come from a wide variety of places throughout Britain and Ireland. In particular, from the 1840s onward the population was swelled by Irish immigrants. The failure of the potato crop and the 'great starvation' had driven many from their homes in search of survival elsewhere. As the main port of entry, the Irish came to Liverpool in very large numbers; some moved on but many stayed. Most of the new immigrants were Roman Catholic, and within a very short space of time, it became clear that the existing churches of St. Mary's, St. Joseph's and St. Anthony's were not able to serve the needs of the densely populated north end. In October 1848, Father Thomas Newsham purchased a piece of land near the docks on which to erect a

St. Alban's church.

new church. Just ten months later, on August 19th 1849, St. Alban's church was opened. Very soon, pressure on housing was so great that people were forced to live in desperately overcrowded conditions, with limited fresh water, inadequate sanitation and little chance of regular employment. Whole families scratched out a bare existence in single rooms. People became caught up in a net of squalor, indignity and deprivation with very little chance of escape. Disease spread rapidly in such conditions.

At the end of May 1887, fourteen women and children from a variety of addresses in Menai Street and Landon Street contracted typhus fever. These included Margaret, Nelly and Cissy Hannaway of 19 Menai Street and Martha, Julia and Kate Morgan of 11 cellar Menai Street. All the children attended St. Alban's school. According to the Assistant Medical Officer of Health all had been infected from a common source:

> "On May 7th, a man named Logan died at Number 23 cellar Menai Street, the neighbours and friends say from fever, Dr. Wild says from bronchitis. A wake [which lasted from the 7th to the 9th May] was held on the body and most of the people recently sick from typhus fever, apprear to have been present at this wake. The children in the house, squalid and prickly, were also ailing at the time."

It's almost impossible to imagine the reality hidden behind such brief comments.

By the turn of the century housing had become very run down. Very few of the dwellings in and around Athol Street had only one family living in them. In some streets, people occupied cellars right up until the blitz. The area was also a centre of industrial activity. Noise, foul smells and pollution added to the misery of those who lived there. Poorly clad verminous, vulnerable to disease and, for the most part hungry, the men women and children of Athol Street scratched out a bare existence less than two miles away from the centre of one of the most prosperous cities in the world.

Nevertheless, welded together by bonds of common misfortune and interdependence, the people of the area established their own sense of identity and worked out the best possible strategies for survival. By the eve of World War I, a closely knit community had evolved, incorporating strong kinship and neighbourhood networks. The years between 1918 and 1939 reinforced the community ties which already existed. Memories of people who lived there then can give us a sense of the background to working-class experiences during that time:

Emily Place - 1897

> "The street was never still. You never had time to get bored there was always something going on from early morning. The streets used to be nothing but people walking to work - dockers, ship's scalers, coal heavers with their shovels, those that worked in the mills, and then the kids out to school . . . women shopping, walking round, up the jigger to put bets on. It was just continuous go from getting up to going to bed."

There was a constant stream of horse traffic which came up from the docks. Overhanging all were the fumes and the smells from the various industries in the surrounding area:

> " . . . Conditions were terrible . . . if Crosfields had a certain fishmeal or what and when the wind was blowing in our direction, you'd get that with the smell of the tobacco from the B.A. Of course we got used to it."

And again:

> "It was a rather smelly area . . . the coke from the fires in the gas works and the smell of the varnish from the Hygena place . . . "

Numerous shops answered all the consumer needs of local people. Shops opened for very long hours. At a time when people's income levels were very low, they shopped by the hour, buying what they needed for a meal, or immediate needs and then going out again later in the day. Some local shops were well-established businesses like Lunt's, and Dan Scully's and Matty Moore's cobbler shop. Cissie Kelly's is well remembered:

> ' . . . She had a big bowl on the counter with a wood lid - a beautiful wood lid, pure white . . . scrubbed white. We could get half-a-pint of milk for a penny and you could sit there all night and you could screech your head off because she was stone deaf. "

Granda' Campbell's marine stores - Athol Street.

Growing up ten years later, Tony Lee had vivid memories of the same shop: " . . . they used to make their own ice-cream and it was out of this world . . . Honest to God, I've never tasted anything like it . . ." People could carry their Sunday dinner or bread dough up to the bakers to be cooked. Al Gough's bird shop was always busy, up on Stanley Road. His grand-daughter, Ivy Griffin (Gough), recalls being sent as a girl along to the knackers yard to fetch 'cat and dog food' in a little wooden cart on wheels " . . . it was still steaming when I collected it!" In brave attempts to improve their family circumstances, some people opened little shops in empty cellars under houses. These carried very little stock and remained open almost all the time " . . . you could go anytime, at midnight, and buy a quarter of tea."

Street sellers added to the variety of life around the streets and courts. 'Lovely Jesus' was an Italian who sold religious statues, and sometimes brought round his budgies that performed tricks and told fortunes for a penny. There were buskers, salt, buttermilk and icecream sellers, and hawkers of every description. Fish Ann, would:

> " . . . have this thing rolled up on her head and a great big basket and she sold fish during the week and on a Sunday morning, she'd come round and she'd shout 'Watercress, watercress, little red things with hairs on'. (laughs) You see, she couldn't say radishes!"

Throughout the inter-war period there was growing concern about the conditions people were living in. Social investigations like those by The Pilgrim Trust and Merseyside Social Survey were uncovering the reality of daily life in dockland Liverpool. In 1935, the Government Housing Act required Local Authorities to carry out a census of overcrowding. These statistics, however, must be regarded with suspicion. Dockland people had much earlier devised their own strategy for avoiding head counts of this sort. Regular inspection of people's houses by 'Night Men' were carried out. This was to ensure that houses weren't overcrowded and that sleeping arrangements separated boys from girls. Families who were found to be overcrowded were liable to prosecution and could have children taken away. The Inspector would arrive in the middle of the night, and demand entry to people's homes. He would use a lamp, and later in the period a torch, to give him light to inspect all the rooms:

> " 'Bang, bang' at the door and they'd put their head through the window and say, 'Who is it?' And he'd say, 'The Night Man'. Well, it was only two bedrooms and a front parlour and a back parlour. We had no back kitchen, only a tap in the backyard . . . So, what used to happen was, they'd shove all the kids out through the midden [the wall bin] and into the house next door while the Night Man did a search: 'Who sleeps here?' and 'Who sleeps there?' Then, when he'd come to the next house, all these kids would traipse back, as well as the kids belonging to that house. They'd all go in and that's the way it was, all up the street. "

Of course, the Inspectors must have been aware of this. People were sometimes prosecuted, but to attempt to enforce the law stringently was futile, given the reality of people's situation. The people of Athol Street took such intrusions in their stride; pulling sleeping children from their beds and out into the cold night to satisfy the needs of a law which condemned the way they lived but offered them no alternative.

The morning would see the streets full again, people going about their business. Men walking down to the docks together, laughing and talking in groups, with little chance of work when they got there. Women folding shawls across their breasts because they possessed no coats and children going down to school in plimsolls or staying home because they had no shoes.

3 A Great Place to Live For Fun

For those children who survived the appalling social conditions and infant diseases endemic to local communities, growing within the north-end docklands could be hard but might also be vibrant and exciting. Most of the people spoken to, who grew up in and around Athol Street recall happy childhoods although the reality of their lives was often dreadful. Coming from large families where money was scarce and housing conditions were for the most part, appalling, children nevertheless developed strategies which made the best of the area in which they were growing up. A young woman who was employed in her first teaching post in St. Alban's School in 1934, described her experiences as an "an eye opener". She came from a working class family who lived in Liverpool but had no idea that people lived in such conditions in the same city. She recalled with amusement, however, the antics of the local children who made the most of Athol Street's position as a main thoroughfare up from the docks:

> "It was the practice of the children, as the carts were coming up, to run out with the breadknife and split the sacks and collect what there was in an enamel bowl or something. There was raw sugar cane up there quite a lot [togy] and the carob beans for cattlefood [known as locusts], sweet and chewy, they used to go for those."

For two of the children themselves, the taste and the excitement of the 'theft' lingers almost seventy years on:

> ". . . And locusts . . . it was like the handle of a knife . . . it was brown and when you chewed it, it was sweet with like little

> beads inside or seeds of some sort and we used to go to the extremes of getting a knife and cutting the bags open, swinging on the carts. " "And run behind it with your jersey and you'd fill your jersey and beat it (laughing)".

Helping themselves from carts and wagons became a universal skill practised by both boys and girls:

> " . . . the horses and carts coming through from the docks with the bales of cotton - we used to rip them open and get a bundle of cotton out for Mum so she could do her polishing - the knocker and door knobs."

In addition children would go round collecting what, quite literally, fell off the back of heavily laden wagons on their climb up the hill from the dock road. However, they weren't averse to helping it on its way where this was possible:

> "In Athol Street there was the Gas Works and the wagons'd be coming in and out every morning loaded up with coke, big, high-sided wagons. As it came out it bumped in a rut in the road and some coke always fell off. We used to swing on the corners as it went down and helped it on its way. We filled a bucket and sold it for tuppence a bucket - that was our pocket money."

As well as tempting delicacies and practical supplements to the household economy, the carts could yield playthings:

> "They used to come through when they was finished through old Hedley Street and up Athol Street, empty wagons, like. All you got was the ropes he had for tying his load up. We used to put them on the lamps and swing on them."

> " . . . and swinging on the lamp, the gas lamps, with a rope on the top. There must have been seven kids on it at a time and (laugh) the lamp swaying from side to side."

Ropes could, of course, be put to use in other ways:

> "It was nothing for mothers to sit on the steps and stretch a rope right across the street for about 20 or 30 kids to play what we called 'Quick Soldiers'. You used to form a big long queue, running in the rope and skipping".

Children scrabbled round back-entry middens for bits of banny mug (broken bits of brown, heavy, crockery) which became 'money' to spend in pretend shops. Anyone lucky enough to find a piece of china ringed with a gold line had found him or herself a 'half-sovereign':

Sherwood Street children - early 1920s

" . . . and if it had two that was a sovereign and the banny mug was your change. You'd use that for money. For your goods you'd find somewhere that they were digging up and you'd get your roll of clay and you'd take it to the steps and you'd make it into all sorts - loaves, everything."

Hop-scotch, tick, kick-the-can and music games like 'The Farmer's in his Den' and 'On the Mountain' are some of the more innocent games recalled:

"We'd be out summer evenings playing rounders or cricket or football between two picked sides at the end of the street getting chased by the bobbies (laughs)".

"Getting chased by the bobbies" for anything from whistling to making slides in the ice in wintertime, was a risk incurred by most childhood fun. Various forms of 'knock-and-run' provided much hilarity but occasionally were quite malicious. Local children growing up in the early 1920s, added an extra dimension to the game, by making their unfortunate target a barefoot street seller, Fish Ann, who lived on the entry in Darwen Street:

"I'd bang at [the] door and we'd run down the entry and along and we'd put all the ashes in the entry, so she'd run along them in her bare feet (laughing)".

As a playground the area was a hazardous but exciting childhood paradise. As Pat McGivern remembers:

"Like everything else when you're a lad, you went the way they all do . . . a bit of devilment. Where I lived Cemeas Street we used to go through old Hedley Street and you were in Lightbody Street and there were all firms: timber yards, ship repairers, the railway yard, it was all handy . . . we used to climb up on the girders after the pigeons".

Many of the houses around Athol Street were propped up by beams which stretched across entries from back to back These provided ideal climbing frames for boys and girls to walk along and swing from. In addition to the risk of drowning, swimming in the canal carried other, less obvious dangers. One ex-reprobate discovered this to his cost when swimming in the 'cut' at the back of New Hedley Street:

" . . . and this policeman came one side and chased us I couldn't get to my clothes so I had to run naked and ran right down Lightbody Street and into the bag warehouse and the women hid me with the bags."

Not all adventures ended so happily, though. Coming from big families

The canal today; the only traffic an occasional pleasure trip

and living in overcrowded homes, children spent much of their free time in the street and were very vulnerable. Little Paul Kelly lost his arm when run over by a Tate & Lyle's wagon in Athol Street. Every year children were maimed and killed. When candles were the main source of light and open fires burned winter and summer to cook food on, as well as to heat the house, accidents were inevitable. In addition, the magnetic attraction of water to children regularly claimed victims. Many more had near misses when rescued by workers from the gas works or other industries located along the canal banks. It would be a mistake though to think that children ran wild and unsupervised. Most of the more exciting aspects of everyday fun were strictly forbidden and carried out without mother's knowledge. Discovery would generally lead to a clout whether from relative, neighbour or policeman. On-the-spot punishment was followed by the near-certainty that the offence would be reported back to parents earning the offender yet another smack. However, in discipline, as in other aspects of local life, there was a clear, if unwritten, code of conduct. There was general acceptance that parents had the right to give their children 'a good hiding' if they saw fit. But persistent or excessive child beating, particularly by men, was openly condemned. The person responsible might well be ostracised or called after in the street.

One little girl, growing up in the years during and after the First World War is still grateful for the help she regularly received from a neighbour:

"I don't know why it was - he wasn't the same with the others - they got smacked but I seemed to get on his nerves and he'd just, like blow up on me. It was the fear of it, not knowing what would provoke him . . . my mother'd get between us or push me out of the door and I'd run, run, run, to my Auntie May's and stay there, sometimes all night, until he'd calmed down. I don't know when I started doing it, but I know I did that for years . . . as fast as my legs would take me."

Violence of this sort was exceptional but it is difficult to generalise. Some children expected to be hit quite regularly, others never remember parents 'raising a hand' to them, ". . . a look was enough!"

The rules governing neighbour's control over children were quite complex. Children were considered almost universal property when it came to running errands: "They didn't ask you, they told you." In the inter-war years, children weren't usually allowed to accept money for running a message, although they might sometimes get a piece of bread and jam as a reward. But no matter how desperate they might be there was one reward that children could easily live without:

"She made Christmas pudding in a great big pillow case and it was dirty grey with all these plums - like a spotted dick only more so. And if you went a message, she'd give you a slice of it, this bloody thing - the weight of it! (laughs) And you'd fall down the stairs carrying it."'

Mouse McGregor's relationship with the children of the area was clearly outside that of most adults:

"Mouse McGregor lived in Mr. Roger's cellar. He had a finger, it was broke, like a hammer. When you were kids your da' used to cut your hair all baldy and just leave a little fringe. He'd say, 'First wet.' and hit you. My God, it didn't 'arf hurt you. Like a hammer."

A woman also recollects:

"Mouse McGregor had a finger, the finger was normal but the top was like a key. He'd say to you, 'Go and get me some bread or something out of your house.' so he could have a meal. And if you didn't go, 'Bang!' on your head, it didn't 'arf hurt. Kids used to go to Paddy's market to steal shoes for him. But when he come home from sea, he'd come out of the pub and then stand on the corner till all the kids come out of school. They'd all walk

> across and say, 'Hello Mouse.' and he'd throw all his change in the road for the kids to get."

Generally, neighbours could 'tell-off' other people's children and even hit them if the offence warranted such punishment. In this latter respect, though, she might be on dangerous ground. The outrage of a mother who felt that a neighbour had overstepped her ground, might easily spill over into violence: "Fights took place, a lot of the time women, and it was nearly always over children. And the next day or two, they'd be back to normal". Such incidents quickly attracted the attention of the whole street. Up would go the cry, "Something to do, something to do!" which accompanied any unusual incident from a spilt load on Athol St. to the discovery of a chimney fire. More children took up the cry as they ran to witness whatever it was that was going on, as on one well-remembered Saturday night in the 1920s:

> "Someone put the rumour out that Katy H. (laughs) had committed suicide - she'd jumped in the canal. And everyone was on the canal bank looking for her, poking big sticks in the water, grappling irons and everything. She hadn't committed suicide at all, she was stood in the crowd looking out. (laughs) "

Life wasn't just one long playtime, though - there was always school.

School Days

In the years between the wars, school loomed large for children between the ages of five and fourteen. Three schools served the children of Athol Street; the Roman Catholic St. Gerard Majella's and the Church of England St. James-the-Less for the top end, and St. Alban's for Roman Catholic children who lived Over the Bridge. In addition there were St. Augustine's and St. Sylvester's further south along Great Howard Street. All were filled to overflowing for the whole period. In St. Gerard's the situation with regard to accommodation was so bad that classes had to be arranged according to ability rather than age.

School played a very big part in the lives of local children. Frank Boyce attended St. Sylvester's but his comments could have been made about any of the schools in the district:

> "The school teachers seemed to spend a lot more time in the area over and above their teaching responsibilities. They would be there at night-time running a youth club or a play centre and running the football team . . . The teachers seemed to know a lot of people intimately, so when I started school the teacher was able to tell me all about my brothers and sisters being there

years before me. They had that long view of people living in the area. They contributed an awful lot to the building up of the community".

This sort of staff commitment is impressive especially when viewed against the backdrop of their work environment. Physical conditions in the schools were far from ideal. St. Gerard's school building was opened in 1914. Despite being overcrowded it was of a relatively good standard. Classrooms were separate, each accommodating fifty children, and were warm and well-lit There were three playgrounds, one each for the infants, girls and boys.

Class 1 St. Alban's school - 1907

The situation in St. Albans, however, was not nearly so good. It carried the dubious distinction of being third on the education authority's list of condemned buildings. The school consisted of one building with three floors; infants on the ground, girls in the middle and boys on top. There were two tiny playgrounds on either side of the building, containing toilets. As early as 1912 His Majesty's Inspectorate for Schools (HMI) criticised the building and the difficulties of teaching in such conditions which were, "potentially very dangerous".

In September 1931, HMI commended teachers for "the work done under circumstances of exceptional difficulty". The school was galleried, there were three classes in the main room. Because of this, teachers had to arrange their timetables so that two classes were quiet while the third had a spoken lesson. Each class contained approximately fifty children. The 1931 Report went on to make specific comments on this situation:

> " . . . [This] must often make it very difficult for the children to hear the teacher and one another and the teacher to hear the children. Training in speaking and work of any kind that involves the use of the voice is seriously hampered . . . and children of this type probably require more of this kind of work than other children from more fortunate surroundings, seeing that they cannot get so much out of quiet work with books or begin to do so early".

Conditions deteriorated over time and by the late 1930s: "The place was overrun with rats. You daren't leave a book out overnight because it'd be chewed up . . . You couldn't have flowers or plants because they'd eat those. "

St. Alban's schoolchildren - early 1950s

Most of the children in school came from poor families and teacher usually had an appreciation of the difficult circumstances they grew up in.

> "The children we had were marvellous children. Although they were poor their mothers did their best to keep them tidy and

that. We never had bare feet, although we would get excuses that they couldn't came to school because they had no shoes. They'd have to wait until some had police clothing or until the money was available for shoes."

Even within such a poor district, though, there were distinctions and degrees of poverty:

"We used to come home for our dinner - there were no school meals. Once, when my dad was away, [at sea] we only had bread for about four days. I remember it well because usually my mum would come up with something or someone round about would. One day my sister was whinging about nothing proper to eat and said she was going to ask for a coupon - my mother leathered her. You see, very, very poor children used to get a coupon to go up to Flinders Street and get a bowl of soup and a piece of bread at dinner time. But they'd run the gauntlet going there because all the kids made fun of them".

Children remained largely unaware of the personal poverty of their families:

"It was just the way you lived, everybody was the same so you didn't actually feel deprived. We all knew kids without shoes, at least I always had shoes even if they were mostly plimsolls, (laughing) pumps they say today. As long as you had something to eat and your own clothes, you didn't think about it."

To have 'your own clothes', even if of very poor quality, was important though. The Police Aided Clothing Scheme provided basic clothing and footwear, (all stamped so they couldn't be pawned) for children without. More than fifty years on, a man recalls his shame at having to wear them:

"I had to wear police clothes for 12 months, when my dad was out of work. My dad went to the parish and they told him to go home because he had a lad working on the bins, he was earning about £3.00 a week and they had to help to keep. So we went to Rose Hill police station and we got rigged out with a brown corduroy suit, grey flannel shirt, a pair of socks and a pair of clogs."

I asked him how he felt about that:

"You felt horrible because the kids poked fun at you, but you couldn't go to school in the nude. As soon as things bucked up they were discarded but nevertheless you had to go. The stench of those corduroys was terrible, you could smell them a mile away and people'd say, 'Oh, aren't they poor?'"

Adults could be equally discriminatory:

> "Cissie . . . and I were great pals at school . . . her dad had a [small business]. When I think about it now, I suppose she had some nice things - clothes and that - well, compared to most of us, anyway ... we was playing round the back when her mother came looking for her. Well she went mad and dragged her home. We trailed up after and we could hear her . . . 'I've told you to keep away from that [her name] . . . no good, none of them!' Well, I was in shock. We all knew who the families were that were no good and ours wasn't one of them. We didn't have much but my mother would of blinded her if I'd told her ... . We kept playing with each other anyhow, but she got a scholarship to the Central and I went to work in the tin factory and we just sort of made new friends, though we always spoke when we saw each other."

Even the local priests aren't exempt from some retrospective comments about their attitudes to local children. Father Dempsey is remembered as . . . a compassionate, laughing man, he always had time for everybody." But elements of bitterness remain in these two accounts of Dean Oldham,

Father Dempsey

parish priest until his death in 1938. A man born in 1912 says that the Dean only made personal visits to those people whose families had shops and small businesses:

> " . . . and if you weren't well-dressed and lovely shoes or lovely clothes on, the Dean wouldn't look at you. I remember the Dean shunning kids like that."

A little girl of the same period felt strongly the same discrimination:

> "The [names of children of some of the more prosperous local families], they could run up . . . they could all put their hands in the Dean's and walk arm-in-arm with him and he'd be delighted, all smiles, waving the walking stick. But you let a poor unfortunate child in its bare feet, which most of us were, go up to him and you'd say 'Hello Father'. He'd either turn his head away or tell you to buzz off. Now that's a fact, that's the truth. But they weren't all like him. Father Hottershall, Father Kelly, Father Clark, they were all lovely."

Children usually had very clear cut ideas about who was and who wasn't 'lovely'. Two other women spoke of the Dean as caring and a source of help and comfort to their families.

Generally, teachers were well-liked and respected:

> "They all had the ability to know your family inside out; every kid - not just you. They knew all your brothers and sisters and what your father's job was and how your mother worked, and how many were in the family."

School provided children with opportunities for doing things that would have been impossible at home. Equipment was limited but " . . . we were never short of exercise book or anything like that. Scratchy old pens [that] you'd dip in ink-wells." Given the inadequacy of the school buildings, physical education could only consist of on-the-spot exercises in the classroom. The Education Committee P.E. Inspector, Miss Hallett, decided that this was simply not good enough, so she arranged to take the children up to a nearby playground for a proper P.E. Lesson. Much to the amusement of local unemployed men who lined the railings, passing comments, the experiment was disastrous The children " . . . just made a dive for the swings (laughs)." Rather more successful was the first time two young teachers took a group of St. Albans girls out for a games lesson. Two years before the War, the Education Committee bought playing fields in Long Lane. It was arranged for schools who didn't have any games facilities, to go out there one day a week:

> "The first time we came, we brought a bus load of girls. They got

> to the field and they emptied out of the bus and there was an enormous yell. 'Oooh grass!' They all tumbled into the field and they just rolled around like puppies. There were no games that day, we just let them."

The Education Committee had also purchased a shop on a street corner opposite the school This was furnished as a house and turned into a domestic science centre, where girls went one day a week:

> "It was good for them really . . . because they learnt how to manage a house and they had a bathroom which they kept in order and used occasionally. There was a bedroom which they had to keep in order and taught how to make a bed properly . . . What had been the shop was the big kitchen where they did the cooking. They also had a little laundry and they got the hang of that."

Such accommodation verged on the luxurious for children accustomed to tin baths, shared beds and washing steaming round the living room fire. Anticipation of school treats created excitement weeks before the actual event. Every year, local traders contributed towards a school party:

> "Joe, the manager of Lunt's donated two bunloaves. Dan Scully, the grocer would donate tins of meat, spam . . . Somebody donated the tea . . . and we would bring our own cup and saucer and spoon and that's the way we would get our school party."

Money was raised from raffles to provide each child with a Christmas present. Tickets cost a penny each and were sold throughout the parish. Again, it was local trades-people who gave the prizes, " . . . a sack of coal from the coal yard, a goose - a real goose, you took it home on a piece of string (laughing)." Children would be given sixpence or a small toy; any remaining money going towards the party. St. Alban's school Log Book records that on May 6th 1935, the children were granted a holiday to celebrate the Royal Jubilee " . . . mementoes in the form of jig-saw puzzles were distributed this morning." In May 1937, a tea-party was held in honour of the new King's coronation, " . . . sixpence per head was allocated by the Committee and each [child] received a certificate."

An annual school picnic, usually to a Wirral beauty spot, was a highlight of the year. Children saved for months before in order to go. They each had a card and when a penny was given to the teacher, it was marked down. By 1936, the total cost of the outing was 2/6. One year though, the eagerly anticipated picnic was turned into a disaster for young Joe Kinsella of Barmouth Street:

> "I cried for a day. We went over to . . . Barnston on the Wirral . . .

And this year I got half-a-crown spending money, I thought I was Rothschild. We all got taken by tram from Great Howard Street to the Pier Head, to the boat and the trams over the other side, to the picnic area And we went to church first, to 8 o'clock Mass and we had to go from there a couple of streets along to where the trams were all lined up and waiting. And when they sent the collection box round, didn't I go and put my two bob in instead of my penny. Oh my God! I was in a terrible state . . . I had a two bob piece and six pennies. When it dawned on me I cried and cried. I couldn't spend nothing all day and I told the teacher about it and she said 'We'll see what we can do'. Anyway they found the two bob piece in the box 'cause nobody put a two bob piece in the box then - they didn't have it. And the next day . . . they found that and they returned it, but it ruined my day out.

St. Alban's choir girls' outing to Southport

Treats, however, were relatively few and far between. School could be a harsh regime for some children One boy never learnt to swim, largely because of the behaviour of one teacher:

> " . . . all the teachers were very good bar one. We got a teacher named Mr. D. and all the kids hated him, he was a bit sadistic in his way. Say you were at the swimming baths, he'd push you in. You could be having a shower and the next minute, he was a big man like, he'd just reach in and you know the cold tap (mimes turning it on), things like that . . . He was a big bully - that was it."

Inoffensive, eager-to-please May Kinsella, spent a very miserable summer morning in the late 1920s. Her mother had made her a sleeveless cotton dress and she'd been sent to school wearing it. The headmistress of St. Alban's, appalled by May's bare arms, slapped her hard and sent her home to cover them up. When she arrived home, her mother with younger children at home which were trouble enough, slapped May for coming home and sent her back to school. For the remainder of the morning the little girl trailed unhappily between school and home, getting slapped and sent back from each in turn.

Clearly though, children weren't always passive victims. A school teacher recalls that "Discipline was very good . . . considering they were cooped up all day." However, children would quickly take advantage if they thought that the teacher was a soft touch'. In April, 1935, the school Log Book records that the Headmaster reported one of his teachers because he was "unable to control his class." In June, 1935, a Senior Class 2 pupil was expelled for "repeated acts of insolence and insubordination."

School truancy wasn't uncommon. Foolhardy senior boys had been known to escape from class by crawling out of the window and across a narrow ledge to the roof of the warehouse beyond. In addition, children might be kept home for a variety of reasons. Girls in particular were expected to help with other children or domestic chores if their mothers were ill or needed to work. Truancy, however, was always rigorously investigated by 'the school board': " . . . Mr. Llewellyn was the school board - a bloody old villain if ever there was one (laughs). He had a terrible look, like a hangman." This image is developed by another child's description of him, "He was hunched over and he always had a grey suit and grey trilby and a beak ready to peck at you. He'd frighten the life out of you."

School ended at four o'clock but the building remained in use until 6.30 p.m. Teachers stayed on to run playcentres to:

> " . . . Keep the children off the streets until the parents had the evening meal [ready] . . . They did things like painting and games, country dancing, ballroom dancing and indoor games like ludo and chess."

Children's lives were very full, "There was always something to do something to see, from getting up until going to bed. It was constantly go." A favourite pastime was looking at the dead. Bereaved famailies thought it unlucky to refuse to let young people in. Children would tell each other about recent deaths in the neighbourhood and they would solemnly call to view the body:

The Nolan children dressed up for Dean Oldham's jubilee

> " . . . And if you couldn't see in the coffin, they'd lift you up (laughs). We were made up. The top of our street a girl had died having a baby . . . and we used to go every day, twice a day, on the way to school and on the way back . . . They must have been sick, weary and tired looking at us. Up the stairs every dinner hour till that girl got buried."

Not all entertainment was quite so morbid, though. In the years following the end of World War I, the 'bagpipe man', a busker, used to come round the streets:

> " . . . and he'd start with one or two kids and he used to make everyone sit down on the floor (laughs) and then he'd march up and down and we'd get up and all be after him and he got so far down the street and he'd turn round quick and every time he'd turn - sometimes he'd just do a quick turn - and oh . . . the screams of the kids! It was a great place to live for fun."

Right in the middle of some of the most appalling social conditions in Britain, surrounded by soot-begrimed buildings and noxious industries, children played and learnt. Despite the reality of their day-to-day lives, what endures is the overriding sense of 'fullness'. Childhood could be brutal but was cushioned by the children's own sense of resourcefulness: "It was a great place to live for fun."

4 Making Ends Meet

The First World War promise of 'Homes fit for heroes', was much more than a moral-boosting slogan. It was an expectation in the minds of those who survived the horrors of World War I and offered some consolation to those who had lost husbands, sons and lovers. Such expectations made the reality of the following two decades even harsher.

Inter-war Liverpool was a place of great contrasts. For those fortunate enough to have regular employment, the period could be one of relative prosperity. New houses, first cars and holidays at the seaside were increasingly part of working-class life. But material progress of this sort left most families untouched. For the mass of the population, dependent on casual work and the shipping industries, times were grim.

Economic depression, particularly visible in the export trades, hit dockland Liverpool very hard. Communities directly dependent on the port were very vulnerable to unemployment. However, although high rates of unemployment were important factors in conditions of poverty and distress, other factors were relevant. Low wages, ill health, large families, old age and the system of casual labour were all crucial. Conditions of poverty, bad housing and poor health were worsened by unemployment but all pre-existed it. Inter-war depression brought severe hardships but for most of the century, Merseyside suffered twice the national average of male unemployment. Casual workers on the docks often used the continuity rules (three on the hook and three on the book) to supplement income by drawing benefit for some part of the week. Therefore, unlike other parts of the country, there was no rigid separation

Liverpool Docks - 1933

of workers and non-workers. Men working in shipping and on the docks, experienced great fluctuations in the availability of work. During the period, the numbers of those seeking casual work on the docks were swollen by men who could not find more regular employment: "My dad had been apprenticed in ship repairing but he was out of work and he had to find work on the docks. When he could that is."

Children finished their formal education at fourteen. A few won scholarships to continue their schooling, but not all of these were able to take advantage of the opportunity. Their parents either did not see the value of an extended education or, much more frequently, simply could not afford to forego the income a fourteen year old could bring in. Fourteen year olds leaving school could usually find some sort of low paid work in 'dead end jobs'. These would he undertaken in the certain knowledge that as soon as the teenagers were sixteen and liable for insurance, they would be replaced by new school leavers. Others might go straight into industry, as one young woman did in 1924:

> "I left school on Friday and went into work on the Monday at Carroll's tobacco place in Greenland Street at 7/6 (37½p) a week. We ended up with 27/6 (£1.37½) at twenty-one. No matter how old you got, it never went any higher. I was stripping tobacco leaves."

52 Latimer Street

Very often, young people needed someone to 'speak' for them in order for them to be employed. Before he went to Canada with the Catholic Emigration Society, " . . . definitely a slave trade", Hughie Holden's uncle, Johnny La Boat got him a job as a boy scaler at the Liverpool Refrigeration Co. Another boy, on leaving school, was employed as a delivery lad at 5/- (25p) a week. When he was old enough, he tried for work at a local cattle food manufacturers:

> "My dad was a boss at Silcock's and he got me a job. He didn't want me to work there, I wanted to go because it was handy. He kept insisting, 'No, if you never have to work, you're not going to work there.' He'd been there fourty-four years and he knew what it was like. It was tough. He was determined he was not going to let me work in those conditions. But I insisted on going and he got me started on the ten o'clock night shift. I was eighteen years old; you couldn't work there until you were eighteen."

Another young man went, at sixteen, to work in Burnell's galvanising plant At that time:

> "Everything was crammed in. All the fumes intermingled and there was a very low roof which made it claustrophobic . . . it was just like Dante's inferno, that's just what it was like. And the carbon monoxide from the coke, sometimes that would be flaming up. Oh God, it was terrible."

The man himself recalls:

> "You could get burnt because when they were actually galvanising, once the object went into the zinc, it'd start splashing. You could be twenty yards away and then the next thing, a big piece of metal would be on your arm and things like that. "

Many local men found employment in the Gas Works. Again this was very heavy, dirty and potentially dangerous work. The employment needs of gas production were seasonal and many workers were laid-off through the spring and summer. It was common for seamen to do one or two trips between April and September and then work the winter months in the Gas Works.

Men and women could seek work in a number of different industries for example, North Shore Mill, Wright's biscuit factory, British American Tobacco, Peerless Refining Company or, "if you had a letter from the

Holy Ghost" for Liverpool Corporation. Invariably, though, what young men and women earned, was turned over to their mother for 'keep' . "In them days you turned your wages up and you got an allowance back off your mum." No matter how small the amount, it could be crucial to the family economy, as we shall see below.

Nelly Courtney of Shadwell Street who worked in Carroll's tobacco works Greenland Street c 1927.

For much of the period, local firms were cutting back and regularly laid-off workers. Increasingly, dole or parish relief were the only sources of income to which dockland families had access. For the women of Athol Street life could be especially hard. Families were often very big: As one man says: "We had seven boys and three girls but ours was just an average family - we weren't big in that street." There was approximately two years between each child which meant that for over twenty years his mother was either pregnant or breastfeeding children. This was far from unusual:

"I don't know how we ever managed as children . . . we had

a very tiny house and there was nine girls and one boy and we only had three bedrooms. So I've never, in the whole of my life, had my own bed."

In Shadwell Street a woman reared twenty two children in two upstairs rooms. Maternal mortality rates were high. Those women who survived were frequently worn down by neglected gynaecological problems and general ill-health. Mrs. Gough, of Wrexham Street also had twenty two children: "She was dead and buried at fifty-four. I'm not surprised. No life, no life and she was an invalid - she had a bad chest."

Women waged a constant battle to care for children, keep their houses clean and find enough money to pay the rent and put food on the table. Making ends meet was one of the greatest problems of daily life. Casual labour associated with the docks, meant that family income was often irregular: "You never knew from one week to the next what you were going to get." The inter-war depression increased the severity of hardships, but irregular income and low wages had long before forced women to develop strategies to ensure the survival of their families. Born of generations of trying to manage, these survival strategies had become part and parcel of daily life.

Even those women fortunate enough to be married to men in regular work were not necessarily better off. They did have the advantage of knowing from week to week what their money was going to be and so could organise their budgets more easily. However, wages were generally low and insufficient to meet the needs of the family.

On top of this, not all men were generous with housekeeping. Men varied in attitude from, "All our wages were put behind the clock, Dad's and all and my Ma gave us back what she thought was right." to "When little Frank was born my sister asked me to go up to meet her fella and get her money off him. She had to do that every week else he didn't bring it home - he was ale house mad. It was humiliating really. I felt ashamed and he wasn't my husband, but it never took a feather out of him." Between these two extremes there were a whole variety of different arrangements. Usually though, women were given, or kept back for themselves, a set amount and the man had the remainder as pocket money.

A lot of a woman's self-respect as a 'good' wife lay in her ability to be a good manager. Given the reality of low and/or irregular income and large families, this could be a totally unrealistic goal. Striving to manage created tremendous strains and anxieties, women endured years of worry and self-sacrifice in order to ensure that husbands and children were fed and clothed as well as possible:

Mrs. Higgins with her sister and children outside No. 1 Barmouth Street

"I don't ever remember her sitting down to a meal with us. She always said, 'I've had mine out the pan.' We never questioned it . . . its only since we've been talking that I've thought that when we were young, my wife never used to sit down. She said she'd had hers with the kids before I came in . . . it makes you wonder, though, now."

Most women left formal paid work upon marriage. A lot of a man's pride was tied up in his ability to keep his wife and family without her going out to work. Men coveted the title of 'breadwinner', no matter how unrealistic this might prove to be. In addition, there was little that was gratifying or satisfying in the sort of industrial work that women did and they were usually quite happy to leave when they married. In any case, even if a woman did want to continue working, very few firms would allow her to do so.

When women are asked if they continued working after they were married or men are asked the same question about their wives, the immediate response is, "No, never". However, this answer is seldom strictly true. Few women went out to work full-time but this is not to say that women did no paid work after marriage. A good many women found work early in the morning or in the evening, cleaning city centre shops and offices. Ships' cleaners worked in gangs, often coming from one street or one or two families:

"Lots of them cleaned the ships, you could hear them - they all had to take their own buckets and scrubbing brushes. And you'd hear the 'army' going down."

This work was very hard and could also be dangerous. Women took in washing both from the ships and from other women who could afford to pay. Assisting in dock canteens provided regular employment for some and might well bring in extra 'perks' over and above any actual money that was earned.

Some women were particularly enterprising in their strategies to bring in extra income. One woman had grown up in a cellar under Kinsella's in Barmouth Street. When she married she moved to Menai Street. To bring in some extra money, she collected wood and then paid local youngsters to chop and bundle it. She would sell it to the corner shop which, in turn, sold it at three bundles for a penny:

"She had a few axes and we would chop the wood into lengths about eight inches. Some would chop and some would be bundling with the string. And we maybe earned sixpence a night with her. Maybe you'd bundle 500 bundles and get sixpence for it."

Sara Grimes, from Hankin Street was:

" . . . continually subsidising the family budget by embroidery. Beautiful work - got buttons for it . . . sideboard runners and duchess sets and things like that. She used to go by word of mouth, she was not a woman who could ask. 'Take that along to your Aunty Kate', it was alright for family, 'and ask her does she want to buy it for 2/11.' And when you came back she could make a meal for that night's tea out of that 2/11. In the meantime she'd be doing something else for tomorrow. And then, Aunty Kate, her friends'd say, 'Ask her to do me one' and so it travelled. It was all done by word of mouth,"

When younger, Sara also worked as a pianist with a trio that played in Bullen's dance hall. Later on, she was able to bring in a little extra by cooking the dinners for St. Gerard's schoolteachers:

"And she'd be embroidering to get the money to get the potatoes and vegetables and whatever it was and she'd make these meals, and my sister used to take them round to St. Gerard's. The headmaster and Miss Lee and Miss Owens had their dinners...she used to get sixpence for the dinner...she was always on to make extra money but it was always from the home."

For seafarer's wives, access to some money of their own was crucial. This could come from work or from the income of adult children. With men away at sea for long intervals, the money allotted to their wives was inadequate, and in any case paid monthly, the situation of these women could be difficult. Even when a man arrived home with his 'pay-off', a substantial proportion of her share would be spoken for. She would have to pay off any outstanding debts in order to maintain her credit worthiness and redeem any goods she had had to pawn. In addition she would have to feed and maintain her husband while he was at home. If very lucky she might be able to buy some necessary items not normally affordable, like children's shoes.

The expectation, intrinsic within dockland culture, was that when a seaman returned to his home port, he 'treated' his friends and male members of his family:

"In those times, when seamen were going to sea, it was a kind of high-class fraternity. If I came home from sea and I'd paid off

Julia Madden photographed outside the house where she worked as a maid, somewhere around the Myrtle Steet area

> and you hadn't a ship, you didn't go short. 'Ere, I'll mug you.' You'd go in and you'd have a night's ale on him."

This sort of brotherly responsibility could mean that when men were home, women were worse off than when they were away. Even if allotments were low they were at least regular and dependable:

> "Oh my God, you never saw them for a fortnight, the dads. It'd be at the end of the street - nearly every street had a pub on the corner - and they'd stay until they were skint and then they'd be looking round for another ship and scrounging off the wife."

In addition, men 'backed out' from time to time. They might jump ship abroad or come into another port and not travel back to Liverpool. In this situation, the plight of wives could become desperate. Apart from the worry of not knowing what had happened to their menfolk, there was the immediate and practical problem of 'no money'.

Of course, not all families had a male breadwinner. The First World War had left many women widowed with young families to bring up. With men working in extremely hazardous occupations, death and serious injury were common: "He was washed overboard . . . months later, she had to go to Ramsey in the Isle of Man to identify him by his watch and the socks she had knitted him." Land based jobs were no safer: "He fell down the hatch and fractured his skull. They got him to hospital but he died anyway." Local people still shudder when they recall the death of one poor man: "He contracted anthrax from a load he was handling and was dead in about six hours."

For widows and single and separated women with dependants, problems multiplied. What was extra income to other women might well be subsistence to them. Also, available work for women was poorly paid and very hard. The local bag and sack warehouses, Marsh's and Boag's, were notorious: "Loads and loads of women used to work there, oh . . . dreadful conditions . . . the conditions were terrible for them."

> "There were returned bags. They used to shake them out and tie or stitch them in tens . . . most of them were hundredweight bags. Now get ten of them . . . I often used to remember this because I was on the docks and we used to get them returned, sacks from Marsh's. I've worked on them a day and maybe a day and a half, loading them into a ship and how the bloody hell some of them women worked carrying them all day, I don't know. They were bags and they were heavy material and they were all hessian. Honestly, they used to get a bundle about [a foot and a half

high]. These were stitched or tied together and the women used to throw them up and stack them high."

Handling and repairing the bags was carried out in an atmosphere heavily polluted by dust and fibres. People from the area are insistent that working and living in such close proximity to such conditions contributed to very high rates of T.B. and bronchial diseases.

Ann Jane Lee of Shadwell Terrace, was widowed in 1934, when three of her younger children were still at school. She had always been "a very hard-working woman . . . She used to go out with the handcart . . . she sold fruit and veg." Shortly before her husband died, Ann Jane opened a little cellar shop under Joyce's in Shadwell Street in 1935, she rented a shop which became the mainstay of the family:

" . . . she took . . . Breen's a barber shop on the corner of Athol Street and Shadwell Street. We moved in there, we lived over the shop and at the back. She sold tea, sugar, sweets, potatoes, cabbages . . . "

A number of women established small businesses to bring in some money on their own account. Some of these survived longer than others. Maggie Duckworth subsequently took over Lee's shop. When she died, Mrs. Donnelly of Shadwell Street, "got the lease". Her docker husband had " . . . got all his lungs burnt in a big fire in the blitz and never worked again."

Women trying to earn a living by shopkeeping were beset by all sorts of problems, especially the necessity of giving credit. Sarah Grimes' husband went to sea for a while and, with the help of his mother, she rented a little shop on the corner of Tindall Street. He warned his wife:

"You'll be able to make a living out of this Sal, as long as you don't give trust! First thing my mother did was give trust, because she said, 'How could you refuse people coming in for a loaf?' So the Trust Book got made out. It was the downfall of their business, really, but it's a very difficult thing not to be able to do. You knew them all and you'd get talked about if you didn't."

Mary Margaret May started her little business in the cellar of her home in Dublin Street:

"My dad was out of work and she started off a little cookshop, ribs and cabbage and roast hearts, ready made dinners, and the kids would come in for rice pudding for a couple of coppers.

Mary Margaret May

Then she began making fish and chips, they were gorgeous . . . and the queues were all outside waiting to get served."

Another local chip shop owner, angry at losing his customers, put in a complaint to the Health Inspectorate because she was operating from a cellar. The Inspector who called to investigate the complaint commended her standards of cleanliness and quality and said he'd support her if she could get other premises. Mrs. May's uncle, John Callaghan, had a chippy at the top end of Athol Street and acquired premises for her further down the street. From there she moved on to Great Howard Street. Small businesses of this sort, though, were very vulnerable. They began with limited amounts of capital and carried very little stock. They relied on quick turn around of stock for profit. People couldn't manage without recourse to 'trust' and many could only shop where it was available to them. Lack of judgement about the credit worthiness of individual people or credit default on any large scale, could quickly close the business.

Whenever possible, women did try to achieve some measure of independence. But no matter how good a manager a woman might pride herself on being, almost inevitably, there were times when she fell into debt. Almost every street had a moneylender. Some of these women could be quite ruthless, charging very high interest rates and terrorising defaulters. The majority, though, provided what women saw as a disliked but essential service. One man recalls being sent by his mother to the moneylenders in the late 1920s and early thirties:

> "Friday night was pay night - debt night, getting your suit out of the pawnshop or paying the moneylender. You would go across to Cissie T. She would do you a good turn, she wasn't one of these loan sharks. If you borrowed a couple of pound off Cissie, you had eleven weeks to pay the twenty two bobs . . . plus the extra two bob for interest ... she was real nice and she'd always give you a couple of coppers if you took over the payment, tuppence for a bag of sweets."

By local standards, two pounds was quite a lot of money to borrow. Amounts could vary but might be as low as a shilling although half-a-crown was more usual. However small the amount, women often felt humiliated at having to borrow from moneylenders or pawnshops:

> "You knew everyone was in the same boat but it didn't make no difference, and it meant that they knew your business. But it couldn't be helped."

A Close Community

In these sorts of conditions, very close communities grew up. Many of the people living in the area were related. Even when someone died, the chances were that the rented house stayed in the same family. Whether related or not, families grew up together, went to school together and later inter-married. In this way close networks based upon mutual support grew up. Women helped each other a great deal: "The community was close as a community. Though you'd argue and squabble one minute, my God, they wouldn't refuse you help the next." Sharing was an integral part of everyday life:

> "I remember one person having a breast of lamb and cutting it up

into chops, slices. And someone would come along and say 'Oh, have you got a breast of lamb?' 'Yes, but I've got bugger-all to go with it. Have you got an onion?' You'd say, 'Yes, but I've got no meat. So the breast of lamb would be cut in half and you would swop. You would give some of your potatoes and veg and she would give you half her breast of lamb. They all did it."

Or, as another woman recalls:

"Everyone helped everyone else. If my mother made a pan of stew . . . nobody had any money . . . and if there was any over, well, nothing was thrown out, it always went to someone else who could eat it."

This sort of relationship was reciprocal. But even people who were outside the net of reciprocity were not ignored. Help was given to those who could return very little in a material sense:

"When she made soup, she'd send me to Johnny Shakeshaft. He lived in the basement of Menai Street. I used to go down Barmouth Street and down the entry. Whatever was left from our meal went round there. And I used to say, 'Derry Walls sent this'."

Help was given as sensitively and unobtrusively as possible:

"My earliest recollections, I can only tell you now, she would never let me tell anybody. On a Saturday morning, my whole morning was taken up taking messages to people who lived alone, little bowls of food wrapped up. I'd go into back entries and into backyards. I remember one in particular, she used to suck a piece of chocolate to keep the hunger from her stomach. They used to literally starve."

Mutual support extended beyond sharing food and understanding:

"If a woman went into labour with her baby, then he [her husband] would be told, in no uncertain manner, by the neighbours, 'You get to work out of the bloody way.' He couldn't afford to lose a day's work. They'd chase him out and they'd get stuck in. They'd scrub the house down and they'd cook the meals for the kids. They'd have his meal ready for him when he came in."

Older women in a street would help at births or assist in laying out the dead: "Somebody'd die, somebody'd come in with the sheets and an old

Catherine Moore of Sherwood Street. c. 1914.

lady'd lay them out. There was none of this undertakers washing them."

Doctors were expensive and people were usually very ill before one was called. Here again a pool of aid and information was available:

> "In any dire emergency, the gas works was the first port of call; first place they came. We had a fully equipped first aid room and a telephone. I saw some terrible injuries, particularly one child hurt on bonfire night."

Older women would advise younger. People had their own 'cures' for almost everything, some of them verging on the tortuous!

> "If you had a rash, your mother smothered your in a mixture of sulphur and margarine and you stunk! If you had scabies or a skin rash or acne, you got smothered in that."

Sore throats and swollen glands' were treated by tying a stocking or sock filled with warm salt around the neck of the sufferer. Children who fell over were told to let the cat lick the resultant scabs. A man, now in his seventies, remembers one scene in particular when the mother of a sick child sought help from his grandmother:

> "It was when the donkeys came round the street. . . I was sitting on the top of the [cellar steps] and some woman came over to her with a sick baby. A donkey's supposed to have a cross on its back it's religious. Well, the mother gave the baby to her and she put it over and under the donkey and said a few prayers. I'd often see her going it after . . . she had all kinds of cures and whatnots."

Hidden within this little tableau, however, is a desperate mother clutching at a slender thread of hope. Infant and child mortality were high. Common childhood illnesses like measles, diphtheria, whooping cough and scarlet fever, were all killers. If a baby or child became ill, all mothers knew that there was real risk that he or she would not get better.

Inadequate sanitation, vermin infested homes, overcrowding and people

St. Alban's schoolchildren

living in such close proximity to each other, created a feeling of futile desperation in mothers. No matter how well cherished and cared for children were, they were still very vulnerable. If children did become ill, conditions added to the difficulties of nursing them back to health. "I was the only girl, she lost the twins in the flu epidemic [of 1918]. She lost the two of them. Only nine days between them, Lily and Mary." A woman recalls: "I birthed eleven and raised five. Mary died having her first baby and the baby died too and then I lost Gerard at Crete. There's just the three of them now." Women were only too aware of the tenuous hold on life that children, especially babies, had. Nevertheless, this knowledge didn't prepare them in any way for the death of the little ones. Decades later, women still mourn their loss in large families, where individual attention was, by necessity, limited, surviving children could even feel jealous of a mother's grief:

> "Not many people reared all their children . . . Christopher and Lucy died within six weeks of each other with scarlet fever. My dad said most of his memories were of the black horses with the plumes. As a child that was a regular part of his life and he used to think, 'Well, one way that my mother will take a lot of notice of me and love me and make a big fuss is when I've got my picture on that wall and when the big horses come and take me away.' She only reared my dad and the youngest, Frank, out of eight children. She lost six in infancy. You can't comprehend the suffering."

Reaching teen years was no guarantee of survival. Tuberculosis was a common scourge. Father Dempsey, curate at St. Alban's, was particularly moved by the illness of one young woman:

> "Little Nellie C. is dying. It is terrible to see an angel dying. She is a little girl of 18, once pretty but now wasted by that scourge of a young girlhood, consumption. Nellie was a favourite of mine since her schooldays. I remember her mother bringing her to me one day to be lectured on smoking and staying out until 11 p.m. She was 15 or 16 then . . . the innocence, purity and goodness of such girls (and I come across a good many of them) overwhelms me with shame and a sense of unworthiness so that I could almost cry . . . it is the deepest tragedy of my work as a Priest..."

How women survived such tragedies with their sanity intact is beyond comprehension. They did receive a lot of understanding and support from other women within their extended families or from friends: "If a woman

Interior Ashfield Cottages

had a problem, every woman in the community had the same problem." Ultimately, though, it was their own strength that carried them through, shadowed throughout by the necessity of daily demands: "YOU just had to get on with it. He couldn't stop home, the kids had to be fed and washed for, the fire had to be made . . . the ashes emptied, you couldn't just stop, you had just to get on with it."

'Getting on' with anything in such primitive housing conditions was, itself, a nightmare. Homes had poor ventilation and were lit by gas or candles. Washing and drying clothes, especially in winter, were major tasks. Keeping a house clean and tidy, without basic facilities such as hot water or storage space, was very hard. In winter, difficulties multiplied; frozen pipes and privies were followed by bursts. Women generally did the very best they could, although it is hardly surprising that a few, overwhelmed by such odds, virtually gave up.

The neighbourhood was over-run with rats. Many houses were infested with vermin. This problem could be so severe that blowlamping bedframes and wiping down with paraffin were largely ineffective. Sitting out in the streets might well be more comfortable:

> "In the summer we were out until all hours. The women'd sit out on the steps and the children would play. The young marrieds would turn the rope for us . . . everybody was out sitting - everybody

sat out; and the bugs at night threw you out! "

As another woman recalls: "We stopped out late - the bugs drove you round the bend . . . My mother used to lime wash the beds and everything but they were in the walls. There wasn't anything you could do."

Sitting out in the summer wasn't merely to gain respite from the bugs, though. Sitting in groups around the steps, women chatted and gossiped, exchanged information and shared companionship and affection. Often this would be combined with mending socks and clothes or, at festival times, making street decorations. Such scenes have an idyllic glow about them which makes it important not to lose sight of the context within which they occurred. Ill-fed, ill-clothed and often in poor health; worn down by hard work and anxiety, the women came up from their cellar homes or out from damp overcrowded houses to snatch what respite they could. They escaped to an environment which was polluted, noxious and dirty. In October 1936, Father Dempsey wrote of St. Alban's parish:

> "The atmosphere is polluted with gases and odours laden with smoke and dust and about as unclean as it could possibly be. The nostrils are invariably caked with black mucous, the throat suffers various afflictions according as the wind blows from the gasworks or the artificial manure factory, and the lungs are constantly irritated and deprived of the pure oxygen they need. Add to this the effect on the nerves of an unwalled barrage of noise from passing traffic, loading and unloading of motor wagons, shouting and singing, a stream of cacophony which continues far into the night . . . "

Against this backdrop women 'made the best of a bad job'. They could share a joke, have a giggle and complain to each other about the difficulties which beset their lives. Underlying all, helping them to make sense of the wearying reality of their lives was the church. Church and community were inseparable; a woman who lived Over the Bridge before the War offers a thoughtful and fundamental explanation of this relationship:

> " . . . People only had this other dimension of the church, really, to give their lives any meaning. Without some sort of faith . . . ? You had to build on some sort of eternity, however incomprehensible it was to you."

As someone else said: " . . . the now was so dreadful that there had to be something better after. Elsewise what would be the point?"

5 Social Life Between the Wars

In the years between the Wars, approximately six thousand people lived Over the Bridge. Of these, there were no more than twenty families who were non-catholic. St. Alban's church was the focal point of the local community. No matter what the parish, though, church was invariably a very important part of dockland life. In addition to its obvious religious significance, many of the young people were members of the various Guilds and Confraternities, a great deal of organised leisure was parish based:

> "Parish really was an extension of the family. Everything that was happening in the church, or the Albany or the school was really part of your own, everyday life . . . The parish, really, was the heartbeat of the whole community."

The Albany club was located on the block between Broom Street and Birch Street. It was here that the Catholic Young Men's Society Club was held (CYMF). This was essentially for men of 18 years upward. Among those who held the position of Secretary of the Albany was Tom Fay, a man highly regarded by the local teenagers:

> "[We played] mostly billiards - they never played darts or anything like that. And we had a very great amateur champion in Tom Fay. He was amateur champion in Liverpool before the War. We boys weren't allowed to go in. We used to sneak in, we've seen him playing you'd get about ten minutes looking at him and then the next minute (laughs), 'Go and play now' and that was it"

Children of Mary on the steps of St. Alban's church

Boys might be able to 'sneak in' but girls had no chance: "The girls used to go crackers, they were never allowed upstairs. Oh my God . . . What? A woman in there! (laughs)".

During the 1930s a meeting place for boys was opened:

> "We had the boys club, as we termed it. That was on the corner of Paget Street. Originally it had been an old pub or something . . . from twelve until you were eighteen. It was a Catholic boy's club."

As well as CYMF, the Albany was a centre for amateur dramatics, whist drives and a variety of social functions.

The church calendar marked out the year for local people. Advent, Christmas, Easter and all the feast days between. The month of May was one of the high-spots of the year:

> "May processions were a real ritual, the crowning of Our Lady's statue. Whole streets, every single house would have something and flowers all around and fairy lights. All the parapets painted white at the end...lamp-posts all silver paper. People'd go down after dark to see the decorations in the windows,"

St. Gerard's May celebrations c. 1937 (front row: Betty Grimes, Hannah Cleary. Kitty Tansy and Kate Woods)

Each year one of the girls would be chosen to crown the statue of Mary, It was a very great honour to be chosen even though parents might well have to put themselves into debt to buy the obligatory long dress and flowers:

> "You had to have the dress and everything. It didn't matter where you got the money from, it had to be better than last years (laughs)."

The chosen one would float estatically on a sea of preparation for months before. But each year lots of children were doomed to disappointment:

> "The only thing I was every disappointed in, I used to go to all the Guild of St. Agnes, the Legion of Marys and yet, I never crowned Our Lady on May Day. And that broke my heart. My sister did, but I never did - not even a handmaiden."

St. Gerard's May celebrations c. 1950 (Joan Grimes and attendants)

Those not chosen could however, walk behind the procession with blue cloaks and white veils over their cótton frocks. In addition, girls could find some consolation in their own, less formal arrangements:

> "At Maytime, we'd make a May procession and get all the kids and take them, all in rags, done up like a queen, along the dock

road up to where the dockers got paid and we'd say 'Help the May procession' and they'd give us money."

Little Winnie Donnelly, more enterprising than most, didn't go to the trouble of organising her own procession:

" . . . And then me and our Betty, we used to watch all the others with the May Procession we used to run in front. We'd be collecting for other May Processions, they weren't ours, (laughs) and we'd get the money and leg it home!"

Feast of Christ the King, St. Gerard's

It wasn't only on major feasts though, that the church became visible within the community:

"The Priests as individuals played a predominant role. They'd go round visiting and checking up on people. As a child I remember being frightened of the Priests, because they did seem to have a lot of authority and power over people."

The Dean, seldom seen without his dog, was regarded with particular trepidation:

"He was a stern man. He used to have a little flat bowler and a big red face, tubby, fourteen stone and he always carried this umbrella and if you were cheeky or if you missed Mass, the umbrella went round your neck and you got pulled to him."

The cry "Here's the Dean" could scatter a toss school much quicker than "Here's the bobbies." The younger priests, Fathers Dempsey and O'Shea were regarded with affection . . . As Mrs. Delia Brannan recalls: " . . . If we were playing cricket opposite the church the Dean'd chase us while Father Dempsey'd say 'Where's the ball?' and join in." It's clear though that Dean Oldham's private face didn't always match his public image. Father Dempsey recorded his regret at the news that the Dean had a terminal illness: "He was a kind and considerate boss."

Local churchmen were generally treated with courtesy and respect. Most people attended Mass each week. The Priests, in turn, had to make allowances for the reality of people's circumstances:

> "They had what they called the Poor Ground because they never used to take the collection box round there. Rather than embarrass them, they probably said, 'If we force the collections on them, they'll stay away from Mass', you know, if they had no money. So the Poor Ground was in the back. And also, women with babies, who would cry and disturb the congregation, would congregate there."

Occasionally, the churches would provide their parishioners with special cause for celebration. One, such event was Father McEvoy's Jubilee in St. Augustine's parish in 1936. Another was Dean Oldham's Jubilee in 1933.

> "When I was about nine or ten years old Dean Oldham had his jubilee and, every street down there, we spent months and months preparing for his jubilee. People were saving every week so they'd have a few bob. The street was decorated every house, to every house, to every house was bunting we all made. Gold, yellow, red, we bought the paper ourselves and all you could see going on for about three or four months before, everybody sat out at night making bunting and flags and lattice work. The handymen in the streets knocked up the lattice work and we, boys as well as girls, we sat up every night making paper roses . . . pink and yellow . . . "

Mary Kinsella, decided that Barmouth Street's decorations were going to rival everyone's:

> " . . . no electricity in those days, all gas. She went down to the electricity board and demanded of them that we wanted lights up for the night of the jubilee celebrations and they put her on to Walker's brewery. There was a pub at the corner of Hedley Street that was known

Window grotto - Regent Street 1937

> as Mick Brennan's and Walker's put the engineers up to take the electricity from the pub, across to our street, and put a wire going across and they were lit for a week at Walker's expense. Three or four days before the celebrations and a couple of days after, while we were winding down."

Dean Oldham toured the parish in an open landau, inspecting the decorations. Then the street parties commenced: "All the adults got tanked up and, as they'd say, 'giving it the bells of Shannon', that's letting yourselves go, while all the kids had their party."

At any time of celebration, street rivalries became paramount and there was great competition to have the most ornate decorations. Such competition overrode considerations of religious divisions:

> "Mr. Doyle was a protestant. He built a beautiful model of Lourdes, with running water to the pool and all the greenery, Our Lady . . . and he had all fairy lights behind it. It was magnificent. Most of the houses had a cellar and some had been filled in with rubbish and concreted over. Well, he had that space beneath his window and he had this grotto on there."

Street decorations to celebrate Fr. McEvoys Jubilee; St. Augustine's parish. Saltney Street court - 1936

Which Side are you on?

In Liverpool at this time, however, not all Roman Catholics and Protestants lived together as amicably as Mr. Doyle and his neighbours seem to have done: "It was part of life. They used to say, 'Which side are you on ? You're not one of them ?' Most of the year we forgot about it but on the twelfth of July or on St. Patrick's day, you knew which side you were on." Nevertheless, even if confined to particular times of the year religious bigotry could and usually did, spill over into violence. There is a common agreement that certain dates were significant:

> "Believe it or not, if any of these people from these different religions were in any sort of trouble, or they were sick, there was no bigotry then. It was only on these specified days that all this would come out . . . The rest of the year they'd forget about it ."

And again:

> "Oh God, it was terrible, absolutely dreadful. We used to stand out by that railway bridge, in Athol Street and throw stones as they were going to Southport. You know, on the twelfth of July, they [the Orange Lodge] used to go to Southport, always and ever. They all had beautiful clothes on for the times, like they do now. And as the trains would be going past, of course they knew it was a Catholic area, they'd throw all the lemonade bottles and everything out through the train windows. Needless to say, night-time, when they were coming back there'd be retaliations. "

'Retaliation' could take various forms:

> " . . . But, don't forget, at the other end, Over the Bridge, they weren't without their little doings as well. They'd have King Billy on a big rope on the twelfth of July and string it across Athol Street. And as soon as the train'd get near, they'd set fire to it and then all the bottles would come out."

Particularly defiant provocation was offered annually by a woman who lived in rooms over a chip shop in Athol Street:

> " . . . her window overlooked the railway line. And every year without fail, every one of her windows went in. Because she was Irish, her name was Nan H. She looked out of her window and the railway tracks ran underneath. And she used to put the yellow, green and white flag out and of course, she paid the penalty every year. But she didn't care. She got every window put in."

Members of the Orange Lodges weren't the only people who paraded. Round the corner of Athol Street, on Great Howard Street there was the Irish Club. A lot of the people who lived in the district were either themselves Irish, or of Irish descent. For some of these, their Roman Catholicism was allied to nationalistic fervour and political sympathy with the 'Irish cause'. In November 1920, the *Liverpool Daily Post* and *Mercury* reported 'Sinn Fein Outrages in Liverpool and Bootle' when a series of fires had been lit along the line of the docks. These were particularly fierce in the north end. Outbreaks of IRA activity in mainland Britain were often followed by police raids Over the Bridge, searching for suspects and weapons.

The vast majority of local people had no actual involvement in such matters but neither did they have a lot of sympathy with the police. When threatened from outside they closed ranks around their own. In the early 1920s, a little girl became unwittingly caught up in a situation not of her making:

> "[Paddy W.] was a lodger in Mrs. Butler's - she lived at the far end of Shadwell Street and there was always police raids for this IRA thing, well, he went missing. He got away from the police and someone must have taken him in. There was a pub, The Red Brick, the corner of Boundary Street and Walmsley Street and I saw this Paddy W. that was supposed to be missing, it was on a Sunday lunchtime. I just said, 'Hello Paddy' he said 'Hello girl' [in an Irish accent]. When I got home they were talking, later on in the night, about Paddy W. 'He's alright, he's got lost'. And I said 'Paddy W. isn't lost"'.

At first disbelieved, when Maggie said where she had seen the runaway, she was packed off to bed. The next day she didn't go to school although there was nothing wrong with her, Her mother took her down to Dr. Brown's surgery and as soon as it opened she went in alone to speak to him. Then Maggie was called in:

> 'He said, 'You're not well'. I said, 'There's nothing wrong with me'. . . So I was made to run gallop up and down these stairs and by the time I'd finished . . . I was nearly dead. And he said, 'You're not well, you can't go to school'. I must have been off school three or four weeks with nothing at all wrong with me. And kept inside. And children'd come asking, never, never grown-ups . . . how I was . . . They made sure I told no-one that Paddy W. was knocking around. The School Board came and there was doctor's notes. He made the mistake and I paid for it."

The Irish Club on Great Howard Street was a well supported centre of activity. Regular ceilidhs were held: "He was a great step-dancer. He'd get dressed up and go down over the bridge to the Irish Club round the bottom from Athol Street." Membership of the Irish Foresters was a visible way of identifying with Irish roots. Costumes worn for festivals or parades were very elaborate:

> "My brother wore knee high boots and velveteen breeches And the jacket and this hat with the feathers in. My sister had a beautiful cloak - she was in the Daughters of Erin and my mother was in the Daughters of Exile. And she had a white dress with a green cloak which fastened over with these cords and beautiful diamante buckle [on her shoulder] and a black, or green hat with buckles on . . . and they were made in Dublin, in O'Connell Street and sent over. Green velvet and about threequarters of an inch wide, there was this gold braid and every now and then it was done into shamrocks."

Like Orange Lodge parades, Irish Forester marches seldom took place without incident: "We were going up to Ford...to celebrate the Irish martyrs, when all of a sudden they were at us - bricks and stones and a fight broke out, turmoil, utter turmoil." A woman remembers being frightened on one occasion: "I was watching them pass, the beautiful clothes and that and suddenly, I don't know what happened, shouting and fighting and screaming and all chaos. I just ran away from it all as fast as I could."

Policing the community

As shown above, relations with the police weren't always harmonious. Much working-class culture was subject to police 'interference'. The way individual policemen interpreted their duty was crucial to the way in which they were regarded by local people. There was a bridewell at the top of Athol Street, in the 1930s Sergeant Croft lived on the premises as 'keeper'. The police patrolled on foot and most were known by name - either their own or a nickname: "There was Jack Pilliner, Jack Butler, Joe Redhead and Musical - Musical always walked with his hand in his pocket": Musical walked up and down Athol Street for at least ten years and is well-remembered. A number of explanations have been offered about his nickname, the most credible seems to be: "He was called Musical because he was in the police band and he had a harp [badge on his shoulder]"

> "he used to have a slight roll [when he walked]. . . Once, I was in with Mr. Rogers - he had a greengrocers on the corner of Broom Street

- and I was getting served and I looked out of the window and I said 'Oh look, Mr. Rogers, isn't that funny? A policeman walking with his hand in his pocket'. When I walked over I said 'Musical, you've got your hand in your pocket! And he just pulled his hand out quick and [she mimes him giving her a clout] and said, 'I haven't now'. (laughs)."

Everyone spoken to recalls the informality of police discipline: "Joe Redhead and Jack Butler, they'd think nothing of giving you a goalong." And again, "You moved when they told you to move."

"You know, you did nothing wrong. Only had a sing-song on the corner and they'd say, 'It's alright don't run, I know where you bloody live and I know your mother. It's alright Furlong, don't run', and you weren't doing nothing."

Children were resentful of what seemed to be petty restrictions:

"All we'd be doing was either playing jumping over backs and playing with a little tennis ball, football and things like that - we didn't have no caseballs . . . but they still moved you on."

At the same time, there was a recognition that the police themselves were under an obligation to support the law, no matter now trivial the offence might appear to be:

"Just say you were standing on the corner, now if you seen a policeman coming over the bridge, down Athol Street, you automatically moved, you didn't wait for him to come down, he'd say to you 'Move'. And you just walked through the street and he'd carry on by. And by the time he got to the next we'd be back on the corner (laughs). But he was doing what he'd been told, 'Keep the boys off the corner'."

Most times, though, as far as minor offences were concerned, the police were lenient; a smack on the head for children and a warning to adults would satisfy. Where possible they might well "turn a blind eye". A few individuals, however, were notorious for their harsh attitude. Recalling parties which spilled out into the street with music and dancing, a man remembers: "Sometimes you'd get a nark such as the 'mad sergeant'. Sergeant Jones - he'd come and chase you, but more or less they'd just walk past and let them dance away." Another policeman was regarded with hatred by adults and children alike:

"He was known as Hitler because of his moustache and being very cruel, kids playing football in the street, it was nothing for him to take the ball off them and stick the knife in it to burst it."

A great deal of police time and energy went into attempts to deal with what was an integral part of working-class life; gambling. Betting and games of chance were very common. Gambling satisfied a number of different needs. It relieved the monotony and boredom of everyday life, bringing excitement into an otherwise dull existence. It also offered a chance of some windfall gains to boost pocket money or housekeeping. On top of this, those who worked as bookie's runners were able to supplement casual wages or unemployment payments.

Atholl Street police station

In January 1918, the Daily Courier reported that two men had been indicted for "Using 17 Denbigh Street for the purpose of betting." The New Athol Members Club had been under observation for some time and it had been noticed that a large number of people entered in the dinner hour: " . . . as many as five hundred on November 7th 1917 ." The police raided the club the following day. "Evidence of the large business done was shown by the fact that in four days 14,000 bets had been made representing £875." The prosecution stated that the club had been conducted by one of the men for two years and "business was mainly among the poorer classes and was a great temptation to women."

The two most prominent forms of gambling were betting on horses and games of pitch and toss; both were illegal:

"There were a couple of street bookmakers. One of the local ones was Tommy (Cabbage) J. He'd been a seafarer. He was only about thirty-odd and he decided to make a book and he operated from his house in Steel Street. He had runners all over the place. These fellows who were on the dole and trying to make a few bob to keep their families going. We had one, he operated between Menai Street and Barmouth Street, in the back entry, Gerry H. He'd take the bets, a shilling or a sixpenny bet, and at the end of the day you waited for a paper to come round to the results to check whether they'd won or not."

The whole system of placing bets could be quite complex. The 'runner" had to know everybody he dealt with and the name they were known by. Nobody used their real name on the betting slips in case they fell into the hands of the police: "Everybody had a 'nom de plume', either three crosses, Coal, Oxo, Big John . . ." Mid-week bets could be made on credit and settled at the end of the week.

The police waged constant war on bookmakers and their runners, but seem seldom to have been rewarded with much success. Runners would pay someone, often teenagers, to act as 'dousy" (lookout) and warn them if the police approached. Even without much warning, though, the runners could usually rely on neighbourly support to help them escape:

"Occasionally, the police would raid them. One day, the Black Maria came whizzing down and a dozen policemen whizzed out of it along the entry and Gerry hadn't been given the tip-off but he run through the street and he got as far as our house and my dad was standing at the door and Gerry shot up our steps through our house and out the back. When the police got to our door they went to go up the steps and my dad said, 'Not through here, not without a warrant.' You always covered up the underdog, unless he was a wife beater or child beater."

It wasn't only those involved in betting on horses who could rely on this sort of back-up when pursued by the police:

"I think the toss schools were a big thing because we always had one. But people escaped through other people's houses . . . There were certain houses where they knew. You could be sitting eating your dinner and loads of people'd be running through your house, down the back yard and over the wall into the next street and casually away . . . "

Groups of men huddled down on the pavement playing pitch and toss was a common sight:

"A lot of gambling went on. I think most of it was to relieve the boredom rather than big stakes. At the end of every street, when the big lads came out of the pub, there'd be a toss school. They'd bet for money and they'd toss up two halfpennies and the Banker, who had the money in, if he tossed up two halfpennies and they came down heads, he won. If they came down one each it was a re-toss until they finally got it."

Gambling wasn't always confined to the streets. The Derby Club, on the corner of Vescock Street was regularly raided by the police. Less formal arrangements could, however, be organised:

"Every Sunday, for many years, we used to have a card school in the house six or seven of the lads, to save getting troubled by the police, would come in after dinner. The boys'd be playing cards from two-thirty onwards till about four or five o'clock. Mum'd make them knock-off, she'd bring pots of tea and potato cakes. And every hand of cards they played a ha'penny would come off into a box. When they finished there might be fifteen bob or a pound in the box. Well, they'd give her that as a kind of payment for allowing them. So that was always helpful, it would keep you halfway through the week."

Perhaps rather more surprising was the card school that ran for a time on the corner of Tidall Street: "They had this basement in this shop that they opened up as a card school and the biggest customers . . . were the local bobbies." Elaborating on this, the daughter of the woman who ran the shop says:

"Policemen used to be on duty all night. So they used to sneak away and relieve one another and so, to bide the time, they'd play cards. So that card school, I think, was mainly for the police."

Gambling wasn't the only illegal activity which took place in the area. However, as with gambling, local people's ideas of right and wrong didn't necessarily coincide with those of the police. In particular, theft was subject to very different moral perspectives. Men and women worked very hard in appalling conditions for very low wages. They weren't valued or respected by their employers and so owed nothing in return. They and their neighbours lived in poverty, barely meeting their subsistence needs - this was immoral. Any strategies they could devise or utilise to counter that immorality, as long as they didn't physically or emotionally hurt anybody, couldn't be wrong.

Theft from work, or job 'perks' were regarded as filling the gap between what people had earned and what they had been paid. At fourteen years old, one young man had to push a handcart right along the dock road to deliver vegetables. Also he would carry orders in a cane basket slung across his shoulders, all the way up to Hall Lane, and:

> "On Friday and Saturday I had to go to the market and get these big barrels of salt fish and pigs tails and pigs tongues in barrels half full of brine. To the fruit market in town with the old handcart . . . maybe about three barrels of different stuff and from there I had to walk back. I got paid five bob a week. Of course, that five bob - I used to knock the top off the barrels and whip a few salt fish out and pass them into my mother I mean, what could you get for five bob?"

Dockers took things from the docks. This was sometimes made easier by the collaboration of certain dock policemen who would look the other way for a share of the goods. Women who worked on the docks were in a particularly advantageous position because they couldn't be searched. One woman whose husband was disabled by an accident on the docks obtained work in a canteen:

> "Oh, the tins of paint off the ships. She used to say to him the policeman - 'I'm taking soup home, because you know my husband's sick.' And tins of ham and things like that and . . . they'd wrap the sheets round them (laughs)."

In an area surrounded by warehouses, it was inevitable that there would be burglaries: "You used to rob a warehouse, but them days there wasn't the same market for them." Stolen goods would generally though, find their way directly into the community: "No matter what it was they got, they shared out - it wasn't sold. The whole street'd have them, they all got shared out."

A strict moral code underlay all conduct. In many ways the community policed itself. People lived very close together and a high degree of trust in each other was essential: "Robbing from your own wasn't on." A frequently expressed comment is that, "you never locked your door."

> "When we were kids, there was nothing like that, breaking into people's houses . . . You didn't have to break in (laughs) you just walked in, there was no keys to the front door."

People mourn the passing of the sense of security, living in such closely knit neighbourhoods engendered. Of course, people weren't all saints, washing would go missing from lines from time to time. Household robberies were infrequent, but nevertheless did occur:

"There was the odd burglary, the gas meter. They'd go in and do the gas meter and find maybe five bob in it. But there was never any aggravation with it, it was a clean break-in; nobody beaten up in their beds."

In any case, there were practical difficulties for anyone who was bent on crime. Homes were rarely empty, strangers were very easily noticed and streets were always full of people.

Women, in particular, had very strong ideas about right and wrong behaviour and seldom hesitated to make their feelings felt: "There used to be a woman got murdered off her husband but the women'd never let him get away with it, they'd call after him in the street, 'Big man and all that'." Direct intervention by neighbours in issues considered to be 'domestic' was, however, unusual. Relatives living close by though, especially mothers and sisters, might step in if they felt one of their womenfolk was being unjustly treated or physically abused.

Men and women would form their own opinions, also, about the guilt or otherwise of people accused of breaking the law. This is apparent from two incidents, one of which occurred just after the end of the First World War and the other in the early twenties. A seaman lived, when home, in Barmouth Street with his mother and the two of them had been squabbling over a young woman he had been seeing. He was shaving at the time and was threatening to cut her throat if she didn't 'give over'. She 'dared' him to and he did. Local people who remember the incident insist that it was an accident and the result of a 'play fight':

" . . . acting the goat, you know, because he adored her . . . he was just fooling round but he cut her throat, next thing she run out on the steps and the kids shouting 'something to do' and then the ambulance was there to take the mother away and the black maria was there to take the lad. Of course everybody was out for him, there was a petition after went in for him, he adored the ground she walked upon but he got hung just the same."

There is a general agreement that this was a gross miscarriage of justice.

There is a similar feeling about the later incident. A young seaman, Frankie M. had just left a ship and was invited by his shipmate to a party. There was an argument outside the house, a woman hit him and he collapsed and died. There were conflicting rumours flying round but the general consensus was that the woman should have been charged with murder and people were outraged when she wasn't. Presumably, the police who investigated believed there was no case to answer. Nevertheless, his family and many of those who lived in the area made up their own minds about the matter: ". . . she was ostracised, people didn't bother much because he was a nice lad." The incident had a postscript:

> "The day he was being buried - he lived off Boundary Street, his mother was going to have red reins instead of the normal reins [on the funeral horses] red reins for murder, and it was stopped. The police stopped it because there'd have been a riot."

As in other areas, people could be quick to take advantage of heightened political tensions. In August 1919, an inquest was held on Cuthbert Thomas Howlett aged 33 of Skirving Street who had been shot by soldiers during the Police Strike. The Daily Courier reported that:

> "Owing to the looting of a bottling store in Athol Street, two motor lorries containing special constables and military, proceeded to the spot where they found a very hostile crowd assembled and the street was strewn with empty beer and stout bottles. Twenty-five men and women were arrested either in or near the premises."

Apparently, the army and the specials then made its way along to Love Lane where it became caught up in another riot. The people earlier arrested in Athol Street began to cut through the ropes and canvas covers of the lorry they were being carried in. Cuthbert Howlett was shot and killed trying to rescue these prisoners. The inquest recorded a verdict of 'Justifiable homicide'. A woman remembers her mother talking about the aftermath of the police strike: "They were panicking in case they were caught with the stuff [looted from shops and warehouses]. She said that they were melting down sacks and sacks of sugar and pouring it down the drains to get rid of it."

As noted above, attitudes towards the police could vary considerably. Some were liked and respected but for the most part they were just tolerated. There was generally an underlying sense of resentment against the police. This was born of generations of what were regarded as petty interferences, that did little or nothing to improve the lot of local people themselves. Coming into the area from outside, they were classified alongside health inspectors, the 'School Board' and a variety of other people who went under the title 'welfare workers'. It was felt that these "outsiders" had little understanding of local life. From time to time, resentment against the police, fired usually by a particular incident, resulted in violence. In Athol Street itself in the early 1930s, two policemen were very badly beaten up: "They got the blokes that did it, though, and they done time for it." Another incident, long remembered happened further along Great Howard Street and concerned two policemen, Dick K. and George P.

> "They went to stop a fight in Regent Street and that had landings . . . the most terrible thing . . . When the police came - people hated the police, they always have done - and the people poured red hot ashes from the top and they went down Dick K's back and he was severely burnt."

Occurrences of this sort were, however few and far between.

The area did have its irredeemable 'baddies' though: "There were some, they'd be no sooner out of goal than they'd he in again. In for a spell, out for a few months or a year and then they'd be caught again." Petty or hardened criminals weren't the only people who spent time in goal. Drunkeness, especially at weekends was a common feature. There werc ninc pubs along Athol Street but this number was swelled by others in the immediate area. Alcohol, like gambling could provide a relatively cheap escape from the realities of everyday life. There were those who 'never felt the taste of drink' but, generally speaking alcohol was enjoyed by many adults, women as well as men. Drunken behaviour could be a source of amusement to sober onlookers:

> " . . . Kit O. (laughs). Kit'd get drunk and she'd have to get the frog's march when the police would lock her up because she wouldn't stop singing. She was doing no harm to anybody but she wouldn't shut up and the police would arrest her. Well she would lie on the floor and she wouldn't get up. The pubs then closed at ten o'clock and our Betty'd say, 'Come on I'm going to bed'. And I'd say, 'Oh no, let's wait' and Florrie H. [Kit's aunt] would say, 'No let's wait and see Kit getting the frog's march'. It was part of your Saturday night matinee (laughs). Whether she was going to get the frog's march or not, we were there waiting for her. 'Let's wait and see Kit.'"

Other drunken behaviour was less entertaining: "Martin H. used to get drunk and sit on the cellar step and sing 'ninety-nine green bottles, hanging on the wall(laughs).' All night. And people used to come out and throw everything at him." But the social problems related to alcohol abuse were also visible, anti-social behaviour, violence and degenerative disease.

Most social occasions, from wakes to weddings, were accompanied by alcohol. This liberal attitude to drink could be a source of embarrassment to young people who were encouraged by school and church to abhor the evils of drink:

> "Our family had a lot of parties . . . Saturday nights I used to think it was terrible when I was a kid. I used to feel ashamed of my family. You used to get up and you'd see half glasses everywhere.

It was very easy to have a party because all you needed was your own family because it was so vast. A few close friends and a few hangers-on and entertainment at their finger tips."

Giving it the Bells of Shannon

To a large extent people created their own entertainment. Music and singing was an important part of this: " . . . They'd have music in the street when they came home from sea and paid off. Beautiful music . . ." A woman from Shadwell Street recalls:

"John Reardon used to play the accordion and then there was his ship-mate played the banjo, Banjo Casey, and Bosey Tierney. There were a couple of mandolins . . . beautiful, like a chestnut shape, seamen used to bring them home. And everyone would be out dancing. They wouldn't have a bite to eat and they'd be dancing and laughing and singing. There was always something to sing and laugh about."

Family celebrations were seldom confined to one house: "If there was a wedding or there was a party, well it wasn't just in their house, everybody joined in. The music was out in the street and everybody was out dancing."

Some leisure activities were part and parcel of working-class culture. Pigeon fancying was one of these. Football was an important element in the lives of many. When they could afford it men and boys went to watch Everton and, to a lesser extent, Liverpool play. Like today, some men took the games very seriously: "Cappy M. Used to follow Everton. If his team lost, Mrs. M. used to get to know before Cappy came home and she had to wait in the Presbytery until he cooled off." Barty Grant recalls that the same man " . . . walked to Wembley when Everton went in 1933. Had no money, got in and walked and hitch-hiked home. And when he came home Bob I had painted his door red (laughs)." As well as following the 'big' teams, local men and boys were themselves keen players. Barty Grant is remembered as being especially good but many local lads played for street teams, which often did well in the local amateur leagues.

The cinema was a source of entertainment which became increasingly important during the inter-war years. There were about ten picture houses in the area and the film in each was changed twice a week. A favourite, locally, was the Gem. In the early years, mothers who went to the Gem wrapped their shawls around their babies and took them with them. At that time the 'chucker out' was Mick Gornall. Enraged by the

Darwen Street football team- 1947/48

sound of any baby crying, he would stamp his foot on the floor and shout "in a big booming voice", 'Shut that child up'. Subsequently a notice appeared 'Babes in arms not permitted'! Saturday matinees became very popular with those children who could afford to go. They were seated on benches and as space ran out: " . . . they used to push you up with a great big sweeping brush" to make room for more children. Dancing had always been one of the more vibrant elements of local life but became even more popular in the years leading up to the War:

> "We had various dance halls - we used to call it the Golden Slipper or the Slipper, as they referred to it. And it was over a chip shop on the corner of New Hedley Street . . . Johnny Pharmach's.[sic] We had a dance, only a piano and maybe an accordion and a drummer. From there we went to another old pub on the corner of Townsend Street, in rooms again and from there we moved to the bottom half of St. Alban's Club and that went on for years. There was all kinds of matchmaking being made (laughs)."

Young people could go to the Penny Hops down at the Darwen Social Club or even sometimes further afield up Scotland Road.

Wireless became a very popular and coveted source of entertainment. In houses without electricity they were powered by large heavy accumulators which had to be carried up along Latimer Street to be recharged. Few, however could afford their own sets:

> "I remember someone opening their window and putting their radio so that everybody could hear that famous speech of the King's - where he took over - George VI. Everyone was out standing in the street - you could hear a pin drop and the house full, all listening . . ."

Frank Boyce's father became a real enthusiast:

> "He built his own radio set . . . he had a blueprint which he sent away for in one of those wireless magazines and he constructed it himself. And at that time, we were the very first family in the street to have one. And the day that War was declared, a lot of the neighbours came in for Chamberlain's speech at eleven o'clock. Our front room was full of people and they all listened to Chamberlain's speech."

Life in the streets around Athol Street changed very little between 1918 and 1939. Those who had lost husbands, sons, friends and fathers in the first World War saw a whole new generation of children growing up in the same desperately poor circumstances. It was as if the sacrifice had never been made. Homes fit for heroes never materialised; houses that were unfit to live in in 1913 deteriorated even further over the next twenty years. The war memorial in St. Alban's church was the only tangible reminder of the carnage that had gone and a poignant warning of that still to come.

6 Blitzed and Bulldozed: The Second World War and After

Rumours of the approach of war multiplied as the 1930's slipped away. In the spring of 1938, a crisis was reached and war seemed imminent. In June. the clergy of St. Alban's were asked to become air raid wardens. On September 27th, Fr. Demsey wrote:

> "We are on the eve of war. Germany has given the Czechs until 1st October to yield to the demands of Hitler regarding the Sudetenland. Chamberlain has twice visited Hitler without any apparent success. France is mobilising and we are taking precautions. Gas masks are being fitted in the schools. Anti-aircraft guns are being fixed in position. Everyone is talking about war."

In the school too, anxious preparations were afoot. A teacher recollects:

> "In the 1938 scare that there might be war, they discovered that the place wasn't safe. They decided that the boys needed another exit. So they made a trap door in the room that I was in and there was a stepladder down, right in the middle of my class. The head of the boys found it convenient, if he wanted to consult with our head, instead of going down into the street again, to just come down the ladder in the middle of my class (laughs) "

However, another year of uncertainty followed. By the closing weeks of

August 1939, nerves were frayed to breaking point. As Fr. Dempsey recorded:

> "Every country is feverishly preparing for the catastrophe. The Baltic and Mediterranean have been closed by the Admiralty to British shipping; every country is calling its ships home, children at home are rehearsing their evacuation and the balloon barrage has appeared over the docks. The newspapers are making as much as they can of it all and everybody has the jitters. And so we wait, wait for news, wait for the wireless, wait for the air raids and the horror to start."

War was at last declared on September 3rd 1939. Preparations for war had been undertaken in the belief that immediate and widespread bombing of British cities would follow. The Government expected that panic would lead to a mass exodus from the industrial areas and evacuation was planned as a means to control this. Most of the children who attended local schools were evacuated to Shropshire. Journeys were often dreadful:

> "It was terrible, we went from Sandhills and of course, all the children came equipped with sandwiches, bottles of lemonade, bottles of water and it was an old-fashioned train with no corridor. We piled all the children in, locked all the doors so that they wouldn't fall out and off we went. We were a good day getting there and the children were drinking, drinking, drinking. You can imagine what happened!"

Mr Hughes' class evacuated from St. Alban's to Much Wenlock

St. Gerard's evacuees with Sr. Gabriel Julie

The people at the other end were appalled when the evacuees arrived. They knew nothing of the conditions which prevailed in dockland Liverpool. The children were sent away in the best their parents could get together, but many were a sorry sight. Liverpool quickly became known as 'Plimsoll City'.

Although some children remained in the countryside for the duration of the war, the vast majority of them had returned within a few months. "When war broke out, everybody expected the next day to be showered with bombs but of course we weren't. It was what you call the 'Phoney War'." Parents were unhappy about their children being away and when the expected holocaust failed to materialise, they began to bring them home.

Worn down by tension, the black-out and queues for everything, the following months were wearying. With men away in the army and at sea, news of mounting casualties and German successes was increasingly depressing. Air raid warnings multiplied through the summer of 1940 and air attacks on Liverpool increased. In December 1940, an unofficial shelter beneath the railway arches in Bentink Street was hit by an aerial mine. It took several days to get out the bodies of the forty-two people killed there:

> "The air-raid shelter under the arches at Denbigh Street and Bentink Street, that was the first real casualties that we heard about. It killed

> a lot of people . . . the people went down about nine or ten at night to make the tea and bring it up to the shelters. And Mrs. F., she'd sent Jimmy, he was the eldest for the tea while he was out . . . they all died, his mother and his sisters. There was only him and his father left out of his entire family."

The years between have added a humorous edge to the following account of the same night, but the horror and the fear of it all remain vivid:

> "There was only one child missed it because they sent him for a loaf. While he was away, Bang! it went. I was in our house when it happened and I jumped under the table and not a window broke. All under the window-sill, that was blown in, me and John Lynch I said, 'You're scared.' and he said, 'Well what are you doing under the table?' A terrible sensation, you could hear it coming lower and you wonder where it's gonna go. So near . . . "

The May blitz of 1941, hit the area very hard. On the night of May 3rd, a particularly heavy raid devastated much of the area and killed several adults and children. Fires in the Gas works and the factories and warehouses around Athol Street added to the nightmare. The Malakand, an ammunition ship berthed in a nearby dock, exploded and caused much destruction. Bombs destroyed houses in Barmouth Street and the surrounding streets " . . . all one side of Barmouth and Menai got flattened in the eight-night blitz." The following day, a little girl of eleven came down to the area with her brother:

> " . . . the shelter had a crack right in the middle and half of it was on a very slight slope going onto the crater. And all of the people in there were saved. My grandmother's rocking chair was blowing on top of the shelter, blowing in the breeze, and there was a soldier on point duty with a pointed bayonet. And I can still smell the stench of the water on the burned rubble, burned wood; that strong, pungent smell, acrid. And there was a big Wellington boot there that had belonged to one of the firemen, and a woman was passing by and she said 'Is there anything in that love?' I was so young, I didn't realise the horror of it and I went over and picked up the boot but it was empty. And all of those warehouses were all smouldering. Number one Barmouth Street was also gone and I remember looking down at my shoes and crying and sobbing . . . "

That morning, buses arrived to evacuate those people who were still there:

> "There were people wandering . . . and there was an old lady walking about and she had the remnants of some sort of house left and

> she said, 'They won't get me away. They'll have to come and drag me away.' People were just absolutely bewildered."

War irrevocably changed the face of the area. A young soldier, badly injured and invalided out of the army recalls the shock of his return:

> "After the Battle of France in 1940, when I came home there wasn't any difference. But when I came home in 1943, I couldn't take it in like; you couldn't take it in."

Many of the houses destroyed in the war had been condemned as 'unfit to live in' more than thirty years before. This fact, however, did nothing to lessen the grief and shock of those who lost their homes at that time: "They were dead lucky when you think how it could of been, but she was in a terrible state. We'd moved in with her mother's sister and when she died we got the house and it had been her mother's before that." Another remembers: "She'd had pictures above the fireplace of her children who had died and they all went as well." Or the commonly heard: "I've got no pictures or bits of things of my family, they all went in the blitz."

The Docklands Post-war

Many of those who lost their homes in the War were evacuated to outlying districts and never returned. Conditions were bleak for those who were left. Bare wastes of derelict land bore evidence to the devastation that had taken place. The brief euphoria of V.E. Day was quickly forgotten in the daily reality of post-war life. Rationing continued and shortages increased. Jimmy McCarty, who worked at the Gas Works, recalls:

> "After the War, right up until the 1950s, fuel was very short. You should have seen the queue of people, from the gate of the Gas Works way up Athol Street, up to Vauxhall Road, it was terrible to see them, because life was hard enough then without . . . They came with prams, pushchairs, handcarts, anything at all to carry it away. We used to sell them in small lots and it would only cost them a couple of bob."

What housing remained had further deteriorated : "It was really only the wall paper that was holding up the walls" and overcrowding had worsened. Initially, the City Council planned to clear the whole area and move the residents elsewhere:

> "At first the Council had decided to just demolish everything the whole of Over the Bridge, and we'd go to Knotty Ash, Kirkby, things like that. Even in them days, though, the people were fighting against moving. Big John Reardon, he was a great

Around New Hedley Street after the War

> character, a Labour man through and through, and he always said, 'There'll be new houses built Over the Bridge'. He never lived to see these new houses, but he said, 'Over the Bridge will be rebuilt."

The campaign mounted by the residents at that time, did not go ignored. Over the Bridge was rebuilt. In November 1949, Davy Logan M.P. for Scotland Ward, wrote:

> "A complete survey of the Scotland Division reveals the inadequacy of housing accommodation. What with blitz and family growth we are very much deficient in providing new houses annually to equal growth of this densely populated area. We have, through the new Housing Director and the Housing Committee, now arrived at what we think may ease our problem. I have come to an agreement that future buildings in this area shall include houses for small and large families, thus obviating the breaking-up of homes and parishes - just in future transfer from home to home as the accommodation for the family may require."

Procession from St. Alban's Boundary Street in the background c. 1957.

True to its word, the Council built property on one side of Athol Street and people moved across from condemned dwellings over the road. These were in their turn demolished and the land built upon. Families were delighted with their new homes. They were spacious, warm, had hot and cold water, bathrooms and indoor toilets. Some of the houses even had gardens.

Throughout the 1960s, new industries were increasingly located in the new estates on the outskirts of Liverpool. In the immediate postwar period, birth rates soared. As these children grew to adulthood and married, they moved away to seek housing and employment in Halewood and Kirkby. In the years since, the area has become very run down. Economic recession has taken the heart from the Liverpool docklands. Many industries have gone and jobs have gone with them; shops and services have followed. 'Strangers' moved in who " . . . had no feelings for the place," and empty property has become 'hard to let'.

Early in 1987, "The Council dropped a bombshell. They said they were going to clear Over the Bridge and build industrial units." Residents were devastated and many did not want to move. For the elderly, the period which followed particularly distressing. People had campaigned hard to persuade the City Council to build new houses around the existing sound and comfortable homes.

Davy Logan, MP, Scotland Ward.

Coronation party New Hedley Street - 1953

Although there were few visible reminders of the community which existed before the War, the sense of mutual responsibility and caring, which characterised that way of life, endured. Those people who had always lived there felt part of a continuum and reflected values and standards born of generations of having to look out for themselves and for each other.

Barty Grant recollects:

> "It was a thriving parish before the War. You had characters, you had thieves and you had intellectuals. You were all accepted, good or bad, everybody was accepted."

A seventy-nine year old woman says:

> "There's too much of the past. They sit there in the club and everything, I'm as bad, I'm no different. 'Do you remember this? Do you remember that?' We've had our lives and there's no going back, is there? It's these young ones I feel sorry for, they don't even seem to be having any going forward."

There is no going back, but the memories and experiences of these older men and women are invaluable. Through them, we can begin to uncover and understand the motivation, vitality and strength of local people. They make visible the contribution made by successive generations of

Liverpool dockland communities. Today, a tangible reminder of Athol Street has been ensured in the naming of Athol Village where people have rebuilt a new community out of the ashes of the old.

Over the Bridge was unique to those who grew up there. But the story told here is one familiar to many thousands of men and women who were reared in communities along the whole length of the Liverpool waterfront. Divisions around religion, race and ethnicity seem so spurious when we recall that the lives of countless people were rooted in a common experience - that of poverty. In the years before the War, the Italians of the Circus Street area, the Jewish families of Brownlow Hill, the Protestants of Park Road, the African-British of the South End, the Anglo-Chinese of Great George's Street and the Yorkshire men and women who had moved to Garston when the bobbin works relocated, were developing their own strategies to get by based on ingenuity, mutual support and hard work. Underlying all was a zest for life which refused to be crushed by the potentially overwhelming tide of hardship, sadness and appalling social conditions, which characterised the daily hand-to-mouth existence of so many Liverpool families in the forty years between the end of the First World War and the beginning of the Second.